UNDERSTANDING THE LATINX EXPERIENCE

UNDERSTANDING THE LATINX EXPERIENCE

Developmental and Contextual Influences

Vasti Torres, Ebelia Hernández, and Sylvia Martinez

Foreword by Sarita E. Brown and Deborah A. Santiago

Stylus

STERLING, VIRGINIA

Stylus

Published by Stylus Publishing, LLC.
22883 Quicksilver Drive
Sterling, Virginia 20166-2019

Library of Congress Cataloging-in-Publication Data

Names: Torres, Vasti, 1960- author. | Hernández, Ebelia, 1974- author. | Martínez, Sylvia, 1976- author. |
Brown, Sarita, writer of foreword. | Santiago, Deborah, writer of foreword.
Title: Understanding the Latinx experience : developmental and contextual influences / Vasti Torres, Ebelia Hernandez, and Sylvia Martinez ; foreword by Sarita Brown and Deborah Santiago.
Description: First edition. | Sterling, Virginia : Stylus Publishing, LLC., 2019. | Includes bibliographical references and index.
Identifiers: LCCN 2018038205 (print) | LCCN 2019002499 (ebook) | ISBN 9781620367339 (Library networkable e-edition) | ISBN 9781620367346 (Consumer e-edition) | ISBN 9781579223151 | ISBN 9781579223151pbk. ; paper) | ISBN 9781579223144cloth ; paper) | ISBN 9781620367339library networkable e-edition) | ISBN 9781620367346consumer e-edition)
Subjects: LCSH: Hispanic Americans--Education (Higher)--Social aspects. | Hispanic American college students--Social conditions. | Hispanic Americans--Ethnic identity. | Group identity--United States.
Classification: LCC LC2670.6 (ebook) | LCC LC2670.6 .T67 2019 (print) | DDC 378.1/982968073--dc23
LC record available at https://lccn.loc.gov/2018038205

13-digit ISBN: 978-1-57922-314-4 (cloth)
13-digit ISBN: 978-1-57922-315-1 (paperback)
13-digit ISBN: 978-1-62036-733-9 (library networkable e-edition)
13-digit ISBN: 978-1-62036-734-6 (consumer e-edition)

Printed in the United States of America

All first editions printed on acid-free paper
that meets the American National Standards Institute
Z39-48 Standard.

First Edition, 2019

Vasti dedicates this book to both of her families—the Torres-Hill family that always supports her, and her academic family that provides her with constant ideas and constructive criticism. This is also in remembrance of the grandfather of her academic family, Roger Winston Jr.—her mentor and friend who passed away.

Ebelia dedicates this book to her family. She is especially grateful to her parents, Inez and Abel Hernández. Their sacrifices have made everything possible for her. She is also thankful to her academic family: her coauthors, Nydia Flores, Merril Simon, Danielle DeSawal, and Martha Blood. She is also grateful to Dana Michelle Harris and Roberto Orozco for their new ideas. And, last but not least, she is thankful to her better half, Bryan Cortnik, whose support means everything to her.

Sylvia dedicates this book to her family, who always support her educational and occupational endeavors. She is particularly grateful to her biggest cheerleaders at home, her husband, Hector, and her son, Andres. She also sends a special dedication to her parents, Alfredo and Ofelia Martinez, who worked so hard so that she could pursue her dreams.

CONTENTS

FOREWORD

Educators and policymakers have long been aware of demographic projections showing significant increases in the U.S. Latino student population. When we, Sarita E. Brown and Deborah A. Santiago, launched *Excelencia* in Education, there was little discussion of Latinos in higher education, and what discussion there was tended to be deficit based. While knowledge about the representation and performance of Latinos in higher education has increased, the actions necessary to engage today's Latino students and tap their talents for higher education, the future workforce, and civic leadership continue to lag.

The opportunity for institutions to improve Latino student success through intentional strategies that recognize students' strengths and needs is timely. In the United States today, Latinos represent one in five college students, one in four K–12 students, and one in three children younger than five years old. To foster positive change to respond to this growing group of students, we at *Excelencia* translate solid academic research into practical uses and potential tactical strategies for policymakers and college and university professionals. This step supports academic, institutional, and policy leaders who seek to understand the dynamism of the Latino population and engage in the design and development of learning environments that facilitate Latino students' success.

This book provides important and useful information and can serve as a resource. It illuminates the experiences of Latino students by setting the context for an important and timely exploration about what we know and what we can do to engage, enroll, and graduate America's young and rapidly growing Latino student population. The authors' choice to blend analysis of longitudinal data about real students on real campuses in a contemporary way with scholarly methodologies and in-depth consideration of the factors influencing the development of Latino identity provides a robust portrayal. Taken together, the content informs models and institutional practices that can serve these students well and support their academic and societal success. Latino students are and will continue to be a significant proportion of the U.S. student body. Therefore, reviewing the models presented in this book will be useful to professionals in higher education throughout the country.

Higher education professionals recognize that influencing students' postsecondary experiences is challenging and essential work. Shaping a campus climate and creating a positive learning experience is fundamental to the work of increasing Latino student success—a goal we share with the authors. Chapter 4 of this book describes how academic institutions impact how students think of themselves, and chapter 6 illustrates the choices Latino students make about which college to attend, choices during college, and choices after they leave college. Throughout, the authors acknowledge that developing meaningful understanding of the Latino student experience is constantly changing and can be messy. Their analysis of the college pathway for Latino students aligns with ours and underscores the importance of understanding the factors in advancing the success of all students.

Most compelling are the stories students tell in their own voices about navigating the borderlands of home, academia, and the real world. Student reflections on their college experiences and the impact of ethnic identity, self-perception, and beliefs about how being Latino influences their experiences in college offer the readers poignant insights about today's Latino college students.

We agree with the authors' statement that "the meaning of *Latino* is changing as our American culture changes" (p. 104, this volume). What remains constant is the opportunity for higher education professionals to better understand Latino students and their life goals and to connect these students' academic aspirations with the best the academy has to offer. Educators, institutions, and policymakers who are better informed will be better prepared to engage Latino students who, in turn, will strengthen higher education and help shape the country's future.

Sarita E. Brown and Deborah A. Santiago
Cofounders, *Excelencia* in Education

PREFACE

When each of the research studies included in this book began, the intent was always to ensure that the voices of Latino students and adults were represented in the literature within higher education. When Vasti Torres began her longitudinal study, most of the research on Latinx students focused on representation and deficit experiences. As an immigrant and a low-income college student, Torres did not see her upbringing as a deficit and wanted to share how Latinx students develop their understanding of the tensions between their culture of origin and the U.S. culture. She knew that both cultures influenced the college experience in positive ways.

The three authors of this book came together at Indiana University as faculty, graduate student, and collaborators around Latino issues. Ebelia Hernández worked with the longitudinal study funded by a U.S. Department of Education Field Initiated Grant as a research assistant and quickly gained an appreciation for the advantages of considering student experiences in a longitudinal manner. She continues to follow students over time in her own research. As a faculty member, Sylvia Martinez brought a sociological approach to our research and was a collaborator on the adult Latino study. Together we each brought a different lens that both benefited and challenged our work together.

The book is set up to provide more in-depth information about the Latino population in higher education. Chapter 1 provides an overview of Latinos in the United States and explains the use of terms to describe the Latino population. Chapter 2 explains the studies that provide data for the rest of the book and provides short case studies on the qualitative participants in the longitudinal college student study. Chapter 3 explains the lifespan model of Latinx identity development that will frame the discussion in later chapters. Chapter 4 uses both qualitative and quantitative data from the college student study to explain how environment, or context, influences the experiences of Latinx students. Chapter 5 delves into the tension of identity and how multiple identities influenced the experiences of students in the longitudinal study. Chapter 6 focuses on the influences around persistence of Latinx college students in higher education. And finally, chapter 7 provides critical insights into what we wish we had considered and suggestions for future research around Latino identity development issues.

In completing this book we want to acknowledge how graduate students assisted us in our thinking and conceptualizing of ideas. The group of Latina graduate students at Indiana University provided both encouragement and insight into our own ideas. At the University of Michigan, Torres wants to thank Ronnie Rios for helping with the tedious details that comes with completing a book that spans decades of work. And finally, thank you to Stylus Publishing and John von Knorring for his patience and insistence that we complete this book.

Vasti Torres, University of Michigan
Ebelia Hernández, Rutgers University
Sylvia Martinez, Indiana University

I

A UNIQUELY AMERICAN STATE OF MIND

Being Latino In Higher Education

To understand the ethnic development of Latinos, one must begin with an understanding of the term *Latino* and why this group is important to higher education in the United States. For this reason, we begin this book with an overview of the term *Latino*, the status of Latinos in the United States, and how these factors influence the identity of the many types of people who make up this ethnic group.

Though there is much controversy over what term to use when one speaks of people from Spanish-speaking countries, the reality is that the term *Latino* is meant to express that the person lives in the United States as a member of the minority group composed of individuals whose ethnic origins trace back to countries that were colonized by Spain. For this reason, Latinos are a uniquely American group of people. Over the past 20 years, much has been written and discussed about the increase of the Latino population in the United States, yet the information presented does not always provide considerable depth or balance. To begin to understand the college experience of Latinos in the United States, one must first understand the characteristics of the population and the barriers that can arise as a result of the trends illustrated in data. This chapter focuses on both the images and statistics that influence how Latinos are seen by others as well as how these data can influence *being* Latino.

Much of the attention focused on Latinos seems to provide images that leave the average person believing that "being Latino" has a singular set of values, behaviors, and background. These depictions, however, lack depth and evidence that would more accurately describe this heterogeneous group of people. Some media reports focus on the growth of the population, while others focus primarily on issues of immigration, with increased attention to issues of undocumented workers within the United States. In other media outlets, the uninformed public is given messages that can lead them to believe that all undocumented workers are Latinos and that all Latinos are undocumented. This potential tension between unstated negative messages and the reality of "being Latino" is the common element among many media reports. Some of the unstated questions that these media reports raise focus on whether there are too many Latinos here, or whether or not Latinos are really contributing to the United States. What few media reports focus on is how poorly the educational system is serving Latinos. While the characteristics that influence the "achievement gap" are talked about in some media outlets (Pérez Huber, Vélez, & Solórzano, 2014; Selingo, 2004), the effort to decrease this gap is limited to a handful of small programs and privately funded initiatives, such as the Gates Scholars Program (Hoover, 2001).

As a starting point, to understand "being Latino" it is helpful to define the term *Latino*. This is a monolithic term that attempts to describe individuals who descended from or were born in more than 20 Spanish-speaking countries located in South and Central America as well as the Caribbean (Garcia-Navarro, 2015; Torres & Delgado-Romero, 2008). Each of these countries of origin has a different history and immigration pattern that influences how individuals can enter and succeed in the United States (Torres, 2004b). We selected the term *Latino* because for many it describes those who are from the "conquered" or "colonized" areas of the new world and therefore share the history that comes with being "conquered" or "colonized." Since late 2014, the term *Latinx* (pronounced La-teen-ex) has become a popular alternative to both Latino and Latina. Its use gained traction among queer communities rejecting the gender binary imposed by the use of Latino/a, Latina/o, or Latin@. Advocates embrace how the term advances social justice for queer and gender-nonconforming individuals. Some critics consider it to be another form of linguistic imperialism; specifically, U.S.-born Latinos imposing new language on predominantly Spanish-speaking Latinos who may struggle to use or pronounce the term *Latinx* (for debate, see de Onís, 2017). For the purposes of this book, we opted to use the term *Latino* when referencing Latino culture or cultural processes more generally, but use *Latinx* when referencing individual students and level aspects of identity. We do so even though our participants did not identify as *Latinx*, because in principle, we believe in the inclusivity the term promotes. On occasion, when we focus on a gender, we use the gendered form of Latino. For those interested in more details about the use of terms, a complete description of the uses of terms to describe Latinos in the United States is available in Appendix A of this book.

The model in chapter 3 of this book illustrates how the societal status of Latinos within the United States influences identity throughout their lives. Societal status is important to understand for two primary reasons. First, society sends messages about which groups have power and which groups are "minorities" and therefore are expected to adapt to the privileged group in power. Constructed cultural beliefs are marked by the social distance between racial/ethnic groups which are considered the norm within the context of a society. This social distance focuses on intermarriage or segregation by group membership and therefore creates differences among cultural groups that are ingrained into the belief system of a society (Magee & Smith, 2013; Quintana, 2007). "It is the culturally invented ideas and beliefs about these differences that constitute the meaning of race" or ethnicity (Smedley & Smedley, 2005, p. 20). These invented ideas and beliefs give rise to racist comments and thoughts.

Second, identity is socially constructed and therefore affected by the ways others view one's cultural group (Erikson, 1959/1994; Torres, Howard-Hamilton, & Cooper, 2003; Torres, Jones, & Renn, 2009). How individuals make meaning of their identity is influenced by how society sees them, therefore making it critical to understanding the context that provokes the social status for Latinos.

To illustrate social status, a series of figures from the U.S. Census and the National Center for Education Statistics (NCES) are presented. These data aim to provide sufficient background about the Latino experience in the United States so that readers can understand the societal context of being Latino as well as the public images that emerge because of these trends. These contextual data will assist you in understanding the stories of the students told in this book. As you will see, the heterogeneous nature of the Latino population requires that one must understand the diverse experiences Latinos have within higher education and that some of these students feel they lack opportunities.

The following sections explain population growth, participation in higher education, and the diversity within the Latino population. From these data one can begin to understand how Latinos receive messages about their social status from the news media and others.

Growth of Latinos in the United States

In the 2000 U.S. Census (2001), the Latino population became the largest minority group in the United States. During this census, *Hispanic* or *Latino* individuals (terms that the Census indicates are used interchangeably) comprised 12.5% of the U.S. population, while Blacks or African Americans comprised 12.3%, and Asian Americans comprised 3.6%. In the 2010 U.S. Census, the continued dramatic growth of the Latino population was evident

(U.S. Census, 2011b). Between 2000 and 2010, the Latino population grew by 43%, four times the growth of the total population, which grew by 10% (U.S. Census, 2011b). In 2014, Latinos comprised 17.3% of the total U.S. population (Stepler & Brown, 2016). The prediction that Latinos would become the largest group was made many years ago, but because this growth occurred faster than expected, it created a buzz within the United States. While being the largest minority group is important to note, what is perhaps more telling is that projections for the future indicate this increase will only become greater (U.S. Census Bureau, 2015). During the 1990s, the population of Latinos tripled in Alabama, Tennessee, and South Carolina and quadrupled in Arkansas, Georgia, and North Carolina (Schmidt, 2003). These are states that are not traditionally thought of as having Latino enclaves, but this trend is changing throughout the United States. While most Latinos continue to live in the West (41%) or South (36%), the most significant Latino population growth between 2001 and 2010 occurred in the South and the Midwest (U.S. Census, 2011). In the South, for example, the Latino population grew by 57%. The Midwest experienced a 49% increase in its Latino population between 2000 and 2010. While growth in the West and Northeast was slower, it was still significant, at about 33% for those areas of the United States. In Figure 1.1, one can see how the Latino population is projected to increase from 14% in 2005 to 29% in 2050, while other groups see modest increases, and the percentage of the overall population that corresponds to White is expected to decrease (Passel & Cohn, 2008). Most recently, projections suggest that by 2060, more than one-quarter of the total U.S. population will be Hispanic or Latino (U.S. Census, 2015).

Though some venues within society embrace the growth of Latinos, it has also brought increased scrutiny to immigration and the assumption that conversations regarding Latinos are primarily about immigration. These messages imply that there are too many Latinos and that they are not welcome in the United States. These are clear negative messages perpetuated in the media on an almost daily basis (Chavez, 2008). In a survey published in *The Washington Post*, it was found that there was bias against Latinos, unless the participant was specifically told that the immigrant spoke English and had a job (Levy & Wright, 2016). The tension between having more Latinos and receiving messages that this is not a good thing from those in power set a context for Latinos to feel unwelcomed and questioned about their immigration status.

Many higher education institutions find themselves serving a growing Latino student population but not understanding the needs of this group. Therefore, this growth in population has not been matched with growth in educational attainment. In many ways the opposite is occurring for Latino students.

Figure 1.1. Projected population of the United States by race and ethnicity.

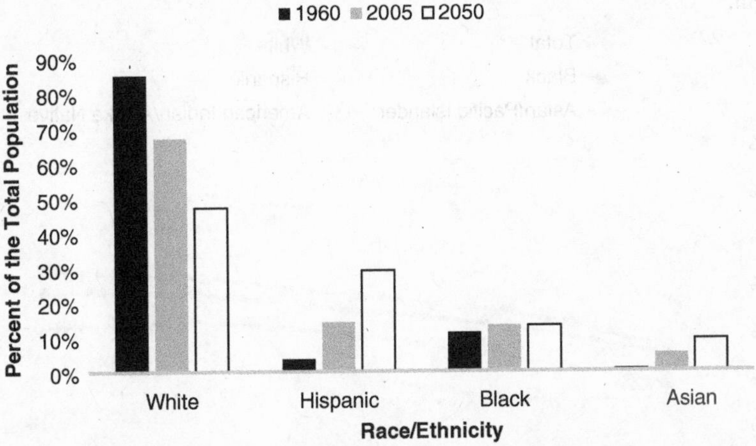

Note: Adapted from Passel, J. S., & Cohn, D. (2008, February). *U.S. Population Projections: 2005-2050.* Pew Research Center.

Participation in Higher Education

Higher education has long been seen as a path to the American dream, yet Latinos continue to lag behind other groups regarding participation and attainment of education. Recent trends show that for the first time, a greater share of recent Latino high school graduates is enrolled in college than Whites (Fry & Lopez, 2012). In 2011, 49% of Latino high school graduates enrolled in college in comparison to 47% of Whites (Fry & Lopez, 2012). And at 16.5% of all college students in the United States, Latinos are now the largest minority in colleges and universities across the country (Fry & Lopez, 2012). These trends, however, still have not led to proper representation of Latinos at the postsecondary level. Considering the percentage of 18- to 24-year-old students enrolled in colleges (including graduate studies), it is apparent that the growth of the Latino population has not translated into equally impressive higher education participation rates. Between 1980 and 2008, Latino participation in higher education increased from 16.3% to 25.8%. This increase pales in comparison to the increase Whites saw in participation between 1980 and 2008—from 27.7% to 44.2%—or Asian Americans, whose participation rates are the highest of any group (National Center for Education Statistics, 2010). Figure 1.2 illustrates the differences in the participation rate of traditionally aged college students within higher education. These data points illustrate that educational systems may not have been ready to receive this growth in the Latino population, and therefore neither the pipeline nor the entry points are working

Figure 1.2. Participation rate in higher education institutions by race and Latino origin.

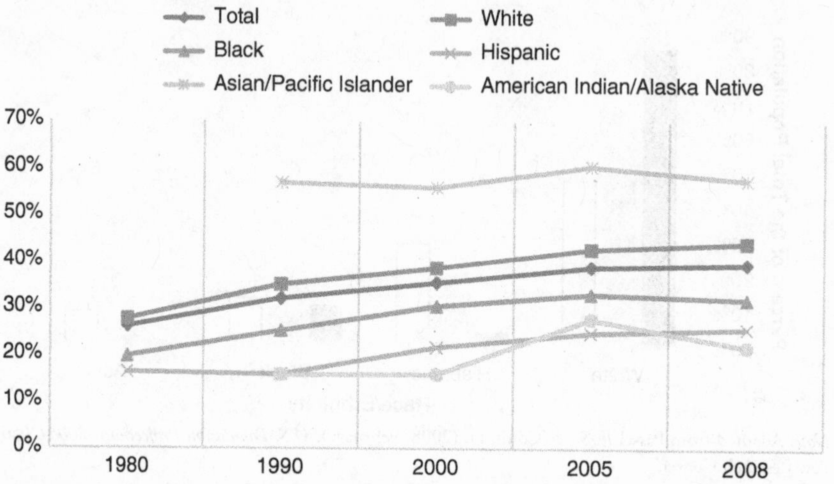

Source: National Center for Education Statistics. (2010). *Status and Trends in the Education of Racial and Ethnic Minorities, Table 23.2* (NCES 2010-015). Washington DC: U.S Department of Education, Institute of Education Sciences. (Public domain.)

Note: Statistics were not collected for Asian/Pacific Islanders or American Indian/Alaska Natives in 1980. In general it is recommended that caution be taken in the interpretation of percentages regarding American Indian and Alaska Natives (Kewal, Ramani, Gilbertson, Fox & Provasnik, 2007).

to lead to participation rates that reflect the proportion of Latinos in the United States. Instead many institutions function without apparent regard for previous educational experiences of the students who are presently attending and soon will attend the institution.

Since Latinos continue to lag behind in participation, the pipeline for educational completion is not very strong. In 2010 13.9% of Latinos had a bachelor's degree or higher as compared to 30.3% of White non-Latinos (U.S. Census, 2011a). To consider whether this gap between Latinos and the majority White group will continue in the future, one can view the degrees conferred during the 2009 to 2010 academic year and see that the gap will continue into the future. Table 1.1 illustrates that among recent college graduates, Latinos received 8.8% of the bachelor's degrees conferred and 13.5% of the associate degrees (National Center for Education Statistics, 2012). To provide parity with the percentage within the population the bachelor's degree completion rate should be at least 12%, or 5% higher than what is being achieved now. A 5% increase seems reasonable to expect, yet this is not happening.

This lack of completion perpetuates the achievement gap and garners additional consequences for Latinos in the United States (Santiago, Taylor, & Calderón Galdeano, 2016).

TABLE 1.1

Percentage of Bachelor's and Associate Degrees Confirmed by Race/Ethnicity in 2009–2010

Race/Ethnicity	*Bachelor's Degrees (%)*	*Associate Degrees (%)*
White, non-Latino	72.9	66.3
Black/African American	10.3	13.7
Hispanic	8.8	13.5
Asian/Pacific Islander	7.3	5.3
American Indian/Alaska Native	0.8	1.2

Source: National Center for Education Statistics. (2012). *Fast facts: Degrees conferred by sex and race, the condition of education 2012, Table A-47-2.* (NCES 2012-045). Washington DC: U.S. Department of Education, Institute of Education Sciences.

The lack of educational attainment influences the level of income that Latinos earn in the workplace. When comparing the mean earnings among racial and ethnic groups, Latinos continue to earn less than Whites. Even when considering those who have earned a college degree, Whites earn almost $9,000 more annually than Latinos and $9,963 more than African Americans. Consistently in every category of degree attainment, Whites earn more than both Latinos and African Americans (Figure 1.3; U.S. Census, 2011a). In fact, the income gap between Whites and Latinos increases as educational attainment increases. The figures show that the largest gap is between Whites and Latinos with bachelor's degrees, and the smallest is for those with less than a high school diploma.

Figure 1.3. Average income by degree earned and race/ethnicity (2009).

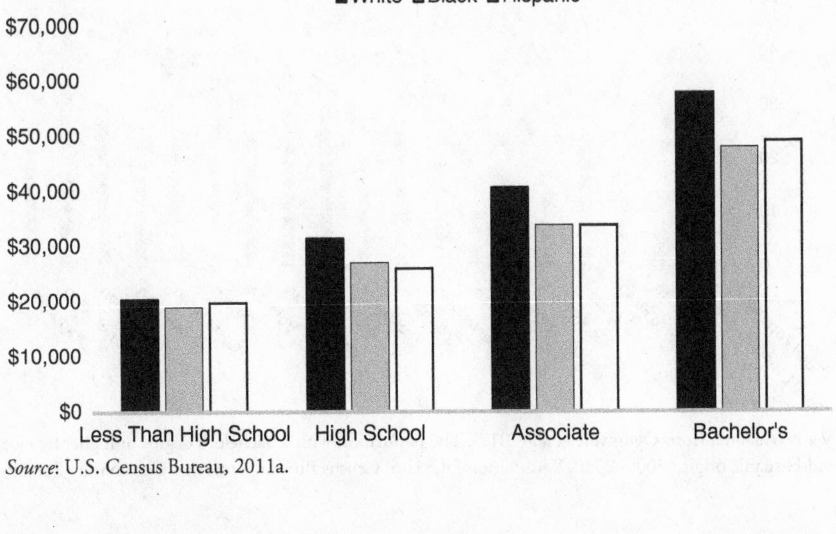

Source: U.S. Census Bureau, 2011a.

Diversity Among Us

When defining *educational attainment* as a bachelor's degree or higher, it is important to view the differences among the different countries of origin represented in the United States. As seen in the previous section, difference in educational attainment can influence economic status as well as other social opportunities. An example of these differences within the Latino population is most noticeable when comparing the highest level of educational attainment, held by those of Venezuelan descent, with close to 50% having a bachelor's degree or higher, to the lowest level of educational attainment, found in those with origins from El Salvador, with only 7.8% having a bachelor's or higher. Figure 1.4 illustrates the great diversity in educational attainment among the countries of origin that are encompassed within the term *Latino* (Ogunwole, Drewery, & Rios-Vargas, 2012).

Figure 1.4 illustrates that Latinos of Salvadoran origin have the lowest level of college-educated people with 7.8%. This rate of college-educated individuals is influenced by issues of immigration and the reasons different populations have immigrated to the United States (Torres, 2004b). Many Salvadoran immigrants in the United States, for example, left their native country because of civil war unrest during the 1980s. One should also note that the largest Latino ethnic group in the United States, those of Mexican descent, also has relatively low educational attainment. The data in Figure

Figure 1.4. Percentage of population 25 years of age and older with a bachelor's degree or higher, by country of origin (2006–2010).

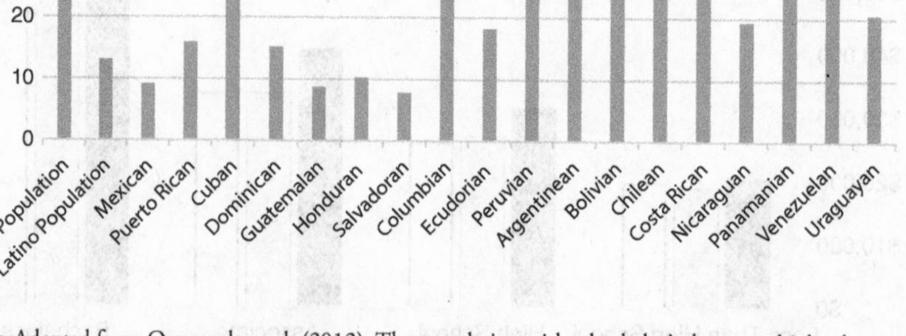

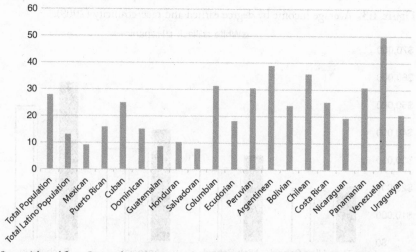

Source. Adapted from Ogunwole et al. (2012). The population with a bachelor's degree or higher by race and Hispanic origin: 2006–2010. Washington DC: U.S. Census Bureau, American Community Survey.

1.4 show that only 9.1% of Latinos over 25 years of age and of Mexican descent hold a bachelor's degree or higher.

What Does All This Mean for Latinos in Higher Education?

There are two major points that are important to highlight in this chapter. First, Latinos are underrepresented in higher education and the gap between those with educational attainment and those without is widening. These data illustrate the "unstated" images of Latinos that are perpetuated—that they are supposed to be poor and poorly educated. For an aspiring Latinx college student or educator to look beyond these depressing statistics, they must be empowered to believe Latinos can be different than what these statistics tell the world. This is particularly true since studies show that Latinos are optimistic about the value of education. Data show that Latinos perceive that obtaining a college degree is important to getting ahead in life, more so than the general U.S. public (Taylor et al., 2009). While 88% of Latinos report education as the key factor for getting ahead in life, only 74% of the general public reports the same (Taylor et al., 2009). Furthermore, Latinos between 16 and 25 years of age are more likely to report that a college degree is important compared to all individuals in that age group (Taylor et al., 2009). Stereotypes and externally defined judgments about Latinos require that educators begin to see their job as myth shattering when it comes to helping the Latinx college student succeed.

The second point is that there is great diversity among this population. Educators need to understand the nuances that occur among this heterogeneous group of college students. The diversity among Latinos is vast and something most educators are unaware of and are struggling to understand and apply to their interactions with Latinos. It is this struggle that this book seeks to address. With so many differences among this monolithic group, how can an educator understand the experiences of Latinos?

Looking Forward

In order to help educators understand and support Latinx college students, this book is set up both to tell their stories and present research analysis that illustrates the choices Latinos make during college and beyond. Chapter 2 provides the necessary background about the longitudinal study and Latino adult study which together form the basis for this book. Chapter 3 offers an overview of how ethnic identity emerged and evolved among the participants of these studies. This lifespan model of identity development is a synthesis of the research conducted through multiple studies.

2

INTRODUCTION TO THE VOICES OF LATINOS

The model presented in chapter 3 provides the synthesized findings from multiple studies focused on the Latino experience. The first two studies focused only on Latinx college students, and the third focused on the adult experiences of Latinos. To understand the importance of and use for the outcomes of studies, here we introduce the research studies and their contextual influences. Methodological considerations are largely explained in Appendix B. This chapter also provides introductions to the sample of participants and institutional context. At the end, we describe the multiple voices included in the findings in this book.

Longitudinal Mixed-Method Study of Latinx College Students

The largest of these studies was designed from an understanding that the decisions made by Latinx college students to stay in college are complex and embedded in multiple contexts with intersecting concerns. While quantitative studies identify generation in college or family influence as two concepts that naturally arise within research studies on Latinos, other factors such as environment, availability of a critical mass of Latinos, and recognition of negative images have not been considered as carefully. In addition, many quantitative databases lack sufficient numbers of Latino participants to include this panethnic group as a variable; therefore, studies may lessen specific cultural understanding by lumping Latinos with other underrepresented/minority groups. The lack of research that considers the complex lives of Latinx college students combined with the lack of longitudinal research on their experiences guided this study.

Previous studies that considered ethnicity as a quantifiable variable inform how practitioners and faculty see the experiences or academic success of Latinx students. However, these studies do not provide insight into how the students themselves see their experiences. For this reason, this study was designed as a longitudinal mixed-method research project focused on the choices Latinx students make to stay in college. The desire to both explain and characterize these experiences required the use of both quantitative and qualitative data to investigate the choices of students within higher education.

Data were collected through three overlapping and complementary studies. The first began at an urban residential, private, research university in 2000; this study will sometimes be referred to as the pilot study. The second study began as a result of a Field Initiated Study grant from the U.S. Department of Education. This study began in 2002 with six institutions, including two community colleges and a private liberal arts college. The survey response rate from the institutions varied greatly, and in the second year of the grant (2003) the scope was narrowed to three urban institutions. Though the narrowing of the sample effectively raised the response rate for the quantitative survey portion, the students who participated in the qualitative portion continued to be tracked with several students from community colleges for the remaining four years. The qualitative data presented in this book include participants from each of the studies who continued to participate in the interview portion, while the quantitative survey data used in this book only include the longitudinal sample from the three urban commuter universities. The third and final study used to inform the findings in this book occurred after the completion of the other two, and it was focused on the meaning-making processes for adult Latinos. This study used a survey approach to explore additional elements of identity development beyond the college years. Because the previous complementary studies were on college students, it was determined that participants needed to be nonundergraduate students or alumni. Therefore, an online open-ended item survey was used, and individuals were recruited from Latino alumni and other Latino electronic mailing lists.

Table 2.1 is provided to assist in understanding the data sources for the synthesis findings provided in this book.

Samples

The largest and most widely used data source in this book is from the longitudinal mixed-method study. For this reason, the samples for each method are presented separately.

TABLE 2.1
Research Studies Included in Synthesis Findings

Research Study	*Number of Institutions*	*Data Collection Years*	*Number of Participants With Multiple Interviews*	*Number of Initial Survey Participants (Response Rate)*
Pilot Study	1 Urban University	2000–2004	9	
Longitudinal Study of Latino College Students	3 Urban Universities (others from year one)	2003–2006	22	2003: 541 (36.7%) 2004: 347 (64.1%) 2005: 240 (68.8%) 2006: 174 (72.5%)
Latino Adult Study	3 Electronic Mailing Lists	2011	Not Applicable	80 (Unknown response rate)

Longitudinal Study Sample

The sample of students who responded to the survey included more females (64%) and a mean age of 20.73 (SD = 5.8). The majority of the students were born in the United States to parents who are immigrants (labeled as second generation—59%), while only 18.4% (100) were foreign born. The remaining students were third generation or beyond in the United States. Approximately 77% of the students were first generation in college, and the majority claimed Mexico as their country of origin, followed by Puerto Rico, Cuba, El Salvador, and other countries. Most students lived with their parents (74.4%), and an additional 19.7% lived in their own home. It is difficult to determine if this sample is representative of the overall census sample at these institutions, because institutions only collect data on ethnicity and not on other demographic characteristics. However, this sample does reflect characteristics of the broader Latino populations in higher education at the time data were collected. In the overall population the largest percentages of students are from Mexican origins (Guzman, 2000; Therrien & Ramirez, 2000) and the largest increase in college attendance is for Latinas (American Council on Education, 2002).

Open sampling technique was used to invite participants from the survey respondents to also participate in the interviews. The students included in this study have been interviewed for multiple years. Some students (9) began their participation with the pilot study in the spring of 2000 (9), some (13) in 2002, and the remaining students (7) began in 2003. All interviews were conducted during the spring semester. A total of 29 students from 4 different higher education institutional contexts are included. There were 19 women and 10 men in the study. The majority of the students were born in the United States (23) and the remaining students were foreign born. Four students transferred and 6 stopped out for at least 1 semester during the 3 to 4 years that they were in the study.

Adult Latino Study Sample

The survey was completed by 93 respondents, but 13 were considered unusable because of incomplete responses or experiences as a college student in the present tense. Of the remaining 80 participants, the majority were women (79%), and most were born in the United States of foreign-born parents (49%). Only 21% indicated they were born outside of the United States. There was a range of educational backgrounds from high school equivalency to doctoral degrees. Most respondents had a master's degree (44%), and the next largest educational attainment group was a bachelor's degree (30%). The age range of the group was 20 to 58 years, with a mean age of 32.4 years.

In the demographic section of the survey, participants were also asked to self-report the representation of Latinos in their communities. Thirty-five percent of the participants claimed to live in communities that do not have a critical mass of Latinos (less than 24% Latino population), whereas 34% of the participants reported living in communities with large Latino populations that comprise 50% or more of the total population. The remaining 31% lived in communities with Latinos representing between 25% and 50% of the population. This distribution of community characteristics provided a diverse contextual sample for consideration.

Institutional Context for Longitudinal Study

The participants in this study were primarily from three urban universities and the university where the pilot study began. For this reason, contextual descriptions of these institutions are provided here.

Monocultural Hispanic-Serving Institution (HSI)

Located in the second largest state in the United States, the monocultural institution had over 90% Latinx student enrollment. The institution was in a city that bordered Mexico, and most of the Latino population was of Mexican descent. This institution will be referred to as the monocultural HSI.

Diverse HSI

Located in an urban area in the Midwest region of the country, this institution's Latino population was approximately 28% of the total student population. It obtained the HSI designation and the student population reflected the diversity among Latino cultures with Cuban, Puerto Rican, Dominican, and Mexican ethnicities. This institution will be referred to as the diverse HSI.

Urban Predominantly White Institution (PWI)

Located in the Western part of the United States, approximately 4% of the student undergraduate population were Latino. Though a low proportion of students, Latinos were the largest minority group at the institution. Located in an urban area, this institution, which will be referred to as the urban PWI, served mainly commuter students.

Highly Selective PWI

Located on the east coast of the United States, this institution was a private research institution with a highly selective student body. This was part of the pilot study and will be referred to as the research PWI.

The diverse contexts where these students experienced higher education provides for a rich description of the Latinx student experience. The stories of the students vary greatly and illustrate a wide breadth of backgrounds and pathways.

Case Studies

To relay the stories of the interview participants from the longitudinal study, a short case study is presented for each participant who stayed in the study for multiple years. The names used are pseudonyms selected by the participants, and every attempt has been made to conceal their identity. These descriptions provide some demographic background about the participants and illustrate the diversity of experiences represented in this study.

Alejandra

Alejandra was born in the United States to parents from Mexico. When she was a child her parents returned to Mexico, where she spent her early childhood. She returned to the United States in her teens, thus giving her a slight accent when she spoke English. She felt the accent was much more pronounced than Torres (the interviewer) would describe it and as a result she felt like she had trouble with the English language and preferred to speak in Spanish. She began the study in 2002 while she was attending a diverse HSI, and she continued as a participant for five years until 2006 when she graduated from college. During the entire time, she lived at home and worked on campus. Her part-time campus job gave her a connection to the university and to staff who made sure she had the information she needed. Alejandra began college as an education major but later had negative experiences that prompted her to change her major to Spanish language and literature. Her motivation for attending college was "to get a good job" because she recognized that her parents did not have the opportunity to get an education and therefore they wanted to make sure Alejandra had the opportunity they did not.

Aldur

Born in the United States, Aldur is a third-generation "American" with a Mexican family background. He was a first-generation college student and began the study in 2002 when he was a freshman at the monocultural HSI. Aldur had many ideas about what he wanted to do but was unable to articulate how he would reach his goals. In his third year of college Aldur stopped responding to requests from the research study.

Andrea

Andrea was born in the United States. Her parents were from Mexico and undocumented. She began in the study in 2003, and was the first in her family to attend college. To help the family Andrea worked 20 to 35 hours a week and attended a monocultural HSI full time. She had taken dual-enrollment courses in high school and enrolled in a vocational career choice program starting in her first year. As a first-generation college student, Andrea lacked information about deadlines and how to maneuver the educational system. By the second year, Andrea was no longer enrolled in school and was working full-time, but she continued to participate in the interviews. Though she hoped to go back to school, she never created a plan that would allow her to complete the degree.

Angelica

Born in the United States to a Mexican mother and Anglo father, Angelica grew up with her mother and spoke fluent Spanish. Her appearance was not stereotypical Latinx, and her last name was not a typical Spanish name; therefore, she had choices about how she was perceived as she progressed through her highly selective, research PWI. After she began as a participant, she transferred to an institution closer to home in her second year of school. This process allowed her to appreciate the environment she had at her original research university, and she returned for her final two years of college. Even when she transferred, Angelica lived on campus throughout her college career, which allowed her to experience a more traditional college life. Angelica finished college in four years and participated in the study for all the years she was in college.

Antonio

Born in Mexico, Antonio began in the study in 2003 while he was a freshman at a diverse HSI immediately after completing high school. Though he was a first-generation college student, he had done very well in high school and was academically prepared for college. However, his family's financial situation required that he work in order to afford college. As an undocumented student, he was ineligible for financial assistance and this made it difficult for him to pay for college and the required textbooks. Though he was part of the honors program, his progress was slowed because of his financial situation. His family obligations also required him to be the primary caretaker for his younger siblings, and this created issues when he needed to study. Though he wanted to go into the sciences and eventually consider medicine as a career, Antonio was realistic about the limitations he had as an undocumented student and changed his major to business. At the end of four years, Antonio was attending as a part-time student because of financial concerns; therefore, he would not graduate for some time. Throughout his college years he volunteered to help pass the Dream Act, federal legislation to help undocumented college students. As of 2018 the Dream Act had still not been passed by Congress, and the study was completed prior to the DACA executive order.

Araceli

Born in the United States of Mexican descent, Araceli was a first-generation college student attending an urban PWI. She lived on campus because her parents had moved to a different state at the time she was starting college. She described herself as a *Chicana* from her first year in college, but later admitted she may not have fully understood what that term meant. She was very involved in a Latinx student group and began college as a Chicano/Latino studies major. By her second year she was overwhelmed by the challenges of being in college and did not seem to have sufficient support to resolve her personal conflicts, which unfortunately led to her losing her scholarship because of too many dropped classes. In her final two years she was managing her stress better and changed her major so that she could use her earned credits more efficiently. She continued to be involved with a Latinx student group and served as a mentor to younger students. By her fourth year in the study she was not going to graduate, but she remained in school. During her time in the study she redefined what it meant for her to be a Chicana.

Bob

Born in the United States of Mexican parents, Bob was in a training program for a health services career. He was a first-generation college student who began in the study in 2003 as a freshman at the monocultural HSI. During the entire time he was in the study, he lived at home because his parents worried about his health. Bob wanted to transfer and go away to college but felt his parents would not let him go away for school. By his third year, he was unmotivated to be in school and his academic progress was slow, yet he did not understand why his peers were graduating with their associate degrees and he was not. Bob remained in the study for three years.

Carlos

Born in the United States of Mexican parents, Carlos began in the study in 2000 when he was a freshman at the highly selective research PWI. Being a first-generation college student, he experienced culture shock when he arrived on campus because he came from a city where Latinos were the majority. College was the first time he had been a minority. In his third year in the study, Carlos explained that he had taught himself sufficient computer skills and he could make more money and be more engaged if he worked full-time. He stopped out of school to work, saying that he would go back and get his degree someday. Carlos stayed in the study for four years, but during that time he did not return to be a full-time student. In his last year in the study, he was reflecting on his own values about education.

Danneal

Born in the United States of Cuban parents, Danneal began in the study in 2003 when she was a first-generation college freshman at the diverse HSI. In her first year, she felt that her high school had low expectations and did not prepare her for college-level work. She participated in an academic assistance program specifically for at-risk Latinos and found the services and information very helpful. As a result of dropping courses, Danneal did not apply to enter the school of education at the expected time, therefore it was not until the end of her fourth year in college that she was able to apply. Perhaps her biggest lesson was to understand that she needed to educate herself about the educational system rather than just assume someone would tell her what to do next. During her college years, Danneal lived at home and did not consider that anything had changed for her.

Diana

Born in the United States of Ecuadorian parents, Diana lived with a family member while she attended a highly selective, research PWI. Her parents continued to live in Ecuador and she worked off campus to help pay for school. By her fourth year, she was working three jobs to make ends meet.

She began in the study in 2000 and struggled to figure out her own choices between the Anglo environment she had at school and the guilt she felt over her family's economic situation in Ecuador. She struggled in school because she had difficulty finding a mentor and felt her faculty did not want to take the time to help her. Despite these negative feelings, Diana found it difficult to ask for help. In her fourth year, she was close to graduating, but would not finish with her peers. She did finish her degree and began working with a nonprofit.

Elizabeth
Elizabeth started the study in 2000 and described herself as half Latino and half Anglo. She came from an area where there were few Latinos, so being at her highly selective, research PWI provided some environmental change for her. Because her father was of Cuban background, Elizabeth had a traditional Latino last name, though her appearance made one assume she was Anglo. Living on campus in her first year she considered herself Anglo-oriented, and her activities were similar to any traditional college student. She found it difficult to have a Spanish surname and not speak Spanish, since people would look at her last name and assume she spoke the language. In her third year of college she chose to study abroad. One of her goals was to learn Spanish and be able to speak to her grandmother in Spanish, which she did. Elizabeth graduated in four years.

Gracie
Born in the United States, Gracie lived around Mexican Americans her entire life and found that her monocultural HSI had more English, or American, culture than she expected. She began in the study in 2001 when she was a first-generation-in-college first-year and used work study to pay for part of her college costs. Though traditional age, she married just before starting college. In her second year, Gracie stopped out because she was pregnant with her first child. While her husband and mother were very supportive of her getting an education and helping with child care, Gracie found it difficult to make the arrangements to return to school. She stayed in the study, even though she was not attending college. In the fifth-year interview, Gracie was pregnant with her second child and had finally made arrangements to enroll in college again. At the time of the last interview, she had registered for a course in the fall, found a mentor/adviser to help her, and was planning to attend full time.

Ivan
A traditional age freshman at the highly selective, research PWI, Ivan was very involved with extracurricular activities, especially those with other

Latinos, during his first year of college. He was a first-generation-in-college student of Colombian descent and came from an area where there was a critical mass of Latinos. Being away from home in this environment provided Ivan with challenges that were sometimes more than he could handle. He began in the study in 2000, and although he selected the bicultural orientation description, he found himself drawn to the Latino activities and student groups. The stress of being in college mounted, and in his junior year he found himself in a situation where he was not taking care of himself. By his final year of college, Ivan had been diagnosed with mental health issues and he was learning how to have more balance in his life. Ivan graduated from college in four years.

Jackie

Having lived in the United States most of her life, Jackie maintained a strong connection to her Puerto Rican background and traveled to the island regularly. She entered the study in 2000 as a freshman at the highly selective, research PWI. Although she grew up in the same city as the university, she lived on campus and was involved in a variety of activities. She was in the school of engineering, which also gave her insight as a woman in a predominantly male field. In general Jackie enjoyed the diversity of her environment and sought opportunities to try new things and learn about different cultures. Jackie never changed her major and graduated from college in four years. After considering several job options, she chose to stay in the area where she had gone to college.

Jebus

As a first-generation college student, Jebus started in the study in 2003 as a freshman at the diverse HSI. His older sister had attended the same university, so he often took her advice on academic matters. Of Puerto Rican descent, Jebus had a very supportive family and worked on campus in an academic department. Because he lived at home, he had few challenges in his day-to-day life. His social circle was fairly consistent from high school throughout college, and he seldom ventured into new activities. He found the people at his work to be helpful in navigating the college system. At the end of four years, Jebus did not understand how some of his high school friends were graduating, yet he still had one or two more years to go.

Juan

Born in the United States of Mexican parents, Juan attended the highly selective, research PWI. He was set on majoring in the sciences as a freshman because his father had encouraged this major. Once he began college, he struggled in the sciences until he followed his interest within liberal arts courses. Juan saw himself as having a bicultural orientation, yet he had few friends who were Latino. During coursework in college he began to discover his own history as a Mexican American and began to associate more with his Latino background. Although he came from a state with a critical mass of Mexican Americans, Juan did not associate with many Latinos until he was in college. At the end of four years, Juan graduated with a liberal arts degree.

Kathy

Kathy began the study in 2002 when a private liberal arts college was included as a research site for the study. Although we ultimately did not collect survey data from this institution, Kathy stayed in the study. Born in the United States, she descended from the Dominican Republic. She was a first-generation college student who had gone away to school to a liberal arts college and lived on campus. Kathy was a Black Latina and talked about the assumptions others would make about her being African American. By her second year, she was living at home and attending a community college in her home state. The main reason for the change had been the cost of attending the institution. She changed her major but could not explain why she chose to do so. In her third year, she transferred again to a local four-year institution and could articulate that it was important that she get her education. She was self-directed in making sure that credits transferred and admitted that the study's annual interviews marked a place of reflection for her. By her fourth-year interview she had stopped out in the fall because she needed to take on more financial responsibility for the household. She was maintaining contact with her adviser so that she could return to college once her financial situation changed.

Lucy

A first-generation college student with Puerto Rican parents, Lucy began in the study in 2002 as a freshman at the diverse HSI. Her family was very supportive of her education, but her father's terminal illness influenced her ability to concentrate solely on her college work. In her second year of college, her father passed away, and this experience caused her grades to drop. After her father's death, Lucy had more time to get to know friends on campus. By her third year, Lucy had stopped out and was considering attending a community college to finish her general education requirements. She worked full time and helped with the family finances while she lived at home. In the fifth-year interview, Lucy was working part-time and trying to help her mother cope with family issues. She still planned to attend college but had not yet returned to being a student.

Maggie

Born in the United States of Mexican parents, Maggie was a first-generation college student who attended the monocultural HSI. She began in the study in 2003 and talked about the cultural conflict she felt between the traditional roles her father expected from women and what she felt she wanted in her life. After a family vacation outside the predominantly Mexican American area where she lived, Maggie experienced a racist incident and this encouraged her to become more involved with student groups on campus. She connected with a mentor who helped her interpret what occurred outside of her monocultural environment. In her third year of college, Maggie was having problems at home and was trying to see if she could transfer and leave home but felt her father would not be supportive of her moving away from home.

Maria

A first-generation community college student, Maria was born in the United States to parents from the Dominican Republic. The community college where she began her college experience had just received its HSI designation and was attempting to reach out to the Latino students in the area. Though the college did not stay in the study, Maria chose to remain and was interviewed by phone. The town where she lived had a critical mass of Latinos—the churches around the town square all had bilingual signs and services in Spanish. Despite the significant population growth in the town, the number of Latinos at the community college barely met the 25% required for the HSI designation. Maria lived at home, and in her first year she believed the stereotypes that indicated Latinos in her hometown were not likely to improve their situation, yet she had been part of the dual-enrollment program at the community college and felt comfortable around Anglos. She eventually transferred to an urban university in the same state, but away from her hometown. The strategies of seeking help and being part of an academic support program helped her succeed at the university. In her fourth year, she was planning to study abroad and understood the influence of her ethnicity on her sense of being.

Martin

A first-generation college student of Mexican descent, Martin began the study in 2002 when he was a freshman at the monocultural HSI. Initially, his intent was to get an associate degree in a medical field, but as the years progressed he became more involved at the university and decided he could finish a bachelor's degree. Martin took advantage of several learning communities, such as supplemental instruction, yet he struggled academically. He became involved on campus and became one of the organizers of cultural trips to different historical sites in Mexico. From time to time, Martin spoke about getting out of his monocultural environment and going someplace more diverse, but at the end of the fifth-year interview he was still living at home and had not completed a college degree. At that point he was exploring transferring to another university to get a joint bachelor's and master's degree.

Mauricio

Born in the United States of Mexican ancestry, Mauricio was a first-generation college student at the monocultural HSI. Mauricio was a respectful and obedient student—this seems to have been influenced by his family situation. Because of his father's disability, Mauricio was responsible for being the caretaker of his younger siblings (the mother was not in the home, although he did try to establish a relationship with her in his later years of college). A committed student, his family obligations were very high, and in his third year of college he lost his financial aid because of insufficient progress toward his degree. This negative consequence caused him to see how he was being influenced by his peers, and he began to spend less time with those friends. By the fourth year of the study, his father's disability benefits had been approved and the financial assistance he was getting enabled Mauricio to concentrate more on his schoolwork. He had also begun to create a network of mentors that enabled him to envision his future.

Melissa

As a first-generation in the United States, Melissa had Mexican parents and attended the diverse HSI as a first-generation college student. She found that the college environment made her more independent and her parents gave her more freedom. Melissa was one of the few students whose parents were supportive and understood that college life could be stressful at times. She worked part-time and understood the importance of seeing her adviser. In her second year, she shadowed an attorney to see if she would like to do that type of work. While there are only two years of data on Melissa, she was one of the few students who was motivated by seeing what was happening to her friends who did not attend college.

Miguel

Born in the United States of Mexican parents, Miguel was a first-generation-in-college student attending the diverse HSI. In his first year he participated in a support program for Latinx students. In spite of this support, he knew he wanted to transfer because his institution did not offer the major he wanted. By his second year he transferred and moved out of his parents' home. His new environment seemed faster paced because of the change to the quarter system. He was a no show for the third-year interview.

Nora

Nora was a first-generation in the United States, with Mexican parents. She was also a first-generation college student who attended the monocultural HSI. Though she lived in the United States, Nora attended a private high school across the border in Mexico. Her images of Americans revolved around them being wild and Mexicans being stricter about what was considered acceptable behavior. Because her precollege academic experiences were conducted primarily in Spanish, she felt like she had some difficulty with writing English, despite her speaking abilities. In her second year, Nora decided that she needed to transfer to complete her major of choice. She used her mentor at the HSI to explain to her father that she could go away to school, but come back home to work once she completed her degree. In her third year, she transferred to the state's PWI flagship campus and found she had to adjust to being a minority for the first time. She had never found herself in an environment where her peers had negative images of Mexicans. By her fourth year, Nora had created a strong support group among other minority students as well as international students. She did not complete her first choice major because of how credits transferred to her new institution. She expected to graduate in five years instead of four.

Panfilo

Born in the United States, Panfilo's parents took him back to Mexico until he was 11 years old. He and his younger siblings then lived in the United States while his mother lived in Mexico. He considered himself head of the household, and this required him to take on more responsibility and mature faster. Panfilo described himself as having a "Mexican heart" and said that he felt only about 10% American. Panfilo attended the monocultural HSI. In his second year he felt overwhelmed by his familial responsibilities and this influenced his academic progress. By the third year, he was able to move the family to a house where he could have his own room, lowering his stress level, but part of this was because he had to stop out to work full-time. At the time of the interview he had just been laid off and was planning to live off credit cards. He was realizing that he needed to have a quick vocational certificate that would allow him some job security while taking care of his younger siblings.

Rosalie

Born in the United States of Mexican descent, Rosalie attended the diverse HSI as a first-generation college student. She lived at home while in college, and her impressions of college life came from TV shows. In her first year of college, she understood that being Mexican came with parents who were very strict and did not allow her to go out. She accepted this as part of traditional Mexican values. Her institution did offer a mentor program in which she participated. By her second year, she was standing up to her parents a little more, but her life revolved around schoolwork and volunteer work. By her third year, she had still not taken the entrance exam to become an education major. She had been part of a cohort, but now her cohort had moved on without her because she still had prerequisite courses to take. This negative consequence taught her that not all courses count and that her cohort experiences did not specifically look at all students' individual requirements.

Sagi

Sagi was born in Mexico, and her parents remained there while she participated in this study. English was her second language, and she was living as an undocumented student in the United States. Sagi attended a PWI community college with plans to transfer to the local PWI urban university. Because of her legal status, she had to pay as she went and could not attend full-time. In her third year in the study, Sagi had stopped out and was working to save money. Although she made progress in speaking English, Sagi chose to do her third-year interview completely in Spanish. In her fourth year, she continued to take one class at a time and work full-time. Her ability to pay for courses limited her progress at the community college. She calculated that it would take her seven years to complete her associate degree.

Sara

Sara was born in the United States, and her parents were from El Salvador. She was a first-generation college student, though her sister was also in college and helped her navigate the environment. She attended the highly selective research PWI and lived on campus. Her parents wanted to maintain strong control over her behavior, even though she lived on campus in a different state. She watched her sister struggle with this level of control and wanted something different. This cultural expectation from her parents was her secret and she did not want other students to know she dealt with this level of parental oversight. By her third year in college, she transferred to a different university closer to home because her parents wanted her to come home on the weekends. Though she was very successful academically and involved on her campus, most of her emotional energy went toward dealing with the cultural expectations placed on her by her parents. In her fourth year of college, she was in a committed relationship but found herself torn between her boyfriend and her parents. Sara completed college in four years.

Sarah

Born in the United States, Sarah had a Venezuelan father and a Canadian mother. Her father passed away when she was young, and she grew up with her mother in the United States. She attended a highly selective research PWI and majored in criminal justice. Just before her first year of college, Sarah visited her father's family in Venezuela, which led her to want to know more about her Latino culture. She got involved with the Latino student group on campus and developed strong social relationships. In her third year, she went on a study abroad trip to an English-speaking country. Upon her return for her fourth year, she kept busy and admitted having little time to reflect. Sarah graduated in four years and went to graduate school immediately after graduation. A couple of years later, she was on the national news because she had been brutally murdered.

Susie

Born in Mexico, Susie's family immigrated back and forth so some of the siblings were U.S. citizens and others undocumented—she was one of the undocumented siblings. She attended the diverse HSI and was part of a special student program at the institution which provided her with specific mentoring/advising. Susie described herself as a former gangbanger and was very clear about what aspects of the Latino culture she liked and what aspects she did not like. She was an undocumented student, so she did volunteer work to qualify for scholarships. As a social work major her desire was to work with inner-city kids who reflected her own upbringing. In her second year, Susie reflected on how she might be called a nerd because she liked to study and was doing well in school. Her family was very supportive of her education and encouraged her. In her fourth year, she switched to be a part-time student. In part, this was because she realized she could only concentrate on a few classes at a time because of work issues. Although she had a good relationship with her adviser, she did not discuss going part-time with her. Susie maintained the same goal of completing her degree but felt this decision was better for her. While she shared that some personal issues had come into play, she did not want to discuss them.

Tristan

Born in the United States, Tristan was a traditional student attending the urban PWI near his home. Because he did not realize the sequence of courses in his major, Tristan missed a year of prerequisite courses he needed to progress. This was the same year that he disclosed his sexual orientation and came out as gay. His parents were not accepting of this and blamed the liberal U.S. society for his identity as a gay man. They discussed returning to their home country of Mexico. Tristan struggled with motivation to stay in college and attempted to change majors as result of his course sequence oversight. Although he wanted to know more about his Mexican cultural roots, Tristan felt more comfortable within an Anglo orientation.

Vanessa

A nontraditional student, Vanessa was born in the United States of Mexican descent. She was married and had 4 children when she began her college career at age 30. Her desire was to become a teacher, and she joined an education cohort in her first year of college at a diverse HSI. When she was younger, she worked to make sure she did not have an accent when she spoke English. Her mother was able to assist with child care while she was in school, and Vanessa found this to be a great advantage because the children were hearing more Spanish—yet they were clear they only wanted to speak English in public. By her third year, the family was able to buy a house in a neighborhood with better schools, and she realized that she needed to ask her adviser more questions about her own academics and her children's teachers about their educational experiences. By her fourth year, Vanessa changed her children's schools so they were attending the best schools they could and her oldest daughter was in a college prep high school. Her father-in-law was now pitching in with transportation for her children. She was also able to reflect that the advising she received in her cohort was not good and this had slowed her academic progress. For this reason, she would not finish with the other students but was approximately one year from graduating. What she learned as a college student had also benefited her children.

TABLE 2.2
Summary of Interview Participants

Pseudonym	*Institutional Type*	*Birthplace*	*Country of Origin*
Alejandra	Diverse HSI	United States	Mexico
Aldur	Monocultural HSI	United States	Mexico
Andrea	Monocultural HSI	United States	Mexico
Angelica	Highly Selective PWI	United States	Mixed – Mexico and United States
Antonio	Diverse HSI	Mexico	Mexico
Araceli	Urban PWI	United States	Mexico
Bob	Monocultural HSI	United States	Mexico
Carlos	Highly Selective PWI	United States	Mexico
Diana	Highly Selective PWI	United States	Ecuador
Danneal	Diverse HSI	United States	Cuba
Elizabeth	Highly Selective PWI	United States	Mixed – Cuba and United States

(*Continues*)

Table 2.2 (*Continued*)

Pseudonym	*Institutional Type*	*Birthplace*	*Country of Origin*
Gracie	Monocultural HSI	United States	Mexico
Ivan	Highly Selective PWI	United States	Columbia
Jackie	Highly Selective PWI	United States	Puerto Rico
Jebus	Diverse HSI	United States	Puerto Rico
Juan	Highly Selective PWI	United States	Mexico
Kathy	Urban PWI	United States	Dominican Republic
Lucy	Diverse HSI	United States	Puerto Rico
Maggie	Monocultural HSI	United States	Mexico
Maria	Community College HSI	United States	Dominican Republic
Martin	Monocultural HSI	United States	Mexico
Mauricio	Monocultural HSI	United States	Mexico
Melissa	Diverse HSI	United States	Mexico
Miguel	Diverse HSI	United States	Mexico
Nora	Monocultural HSI	United States	Mexico
Panfilo	Monocultural HSI	United States	Mexico
Rosalie	Diverse HSI	United States	Mexico
Sagi	Community College PWI	Mexico	Mexico
Sara	Highly Selective PWI	United States	El Salvador
Sarah	Highly Selective PWI	United States	Mixed – Venezuela and Canada
Susie	Diverse HSI	United States	Mexico
Tristan	Urban PWI	United States	Mexico
Vanessa	Diverse HSI	United States	Mexico

Summary

The diverse participants in the longitudinal study provide rich data about both the experiences of these students as well as the choices they made regarding their cultural ethnicity. The variety of participants is summarized in Table 2.2 to assist the reader. While the descriptions in this table and chapter give some specific characteristics about the participants, their voices will be shared in the following chapters.

3

A LIFESPAN MODEL OF LATINX ETHNIC IDENTITY DEVELOPMENT

This chapter presents a synthesis of various research results that led to the development of the lifespan model of Latino ethnic identity development. This type of research is designed around using each of the studies as data, and results emerge when synthesizing (Cresswel & Plano Clark, 2007). Like other developmental models, the lifespan model has several statuses and behaviors that influence movement among the statuses. To introduce the model each status begins with a broad description and explains how choices and meaning-making occur throughout the overall model. The theoretical foundations of the model are grounded in the literature on the development of identity. For this reason, we begin with an overview of the literature on identity and ethnic identity development.

Identity Development

As individuals organize the environment around themselves, their identity begins to be formed (Erikson, 1959/1994). This relationship among environment, others, and self lays the foundation for self-identification and is the reason identity is socially constructed by the culture (context) in which it evolves (Kroger, 2004). This is an important aspect to understand when working with Latinx students; growing up in an area as part of the majority population is different than growing up in an area as a minority with a different language, foods, and customs. Thus, the model presented in this chapter focuses only on those who were raised in the United States and does not describe international students who would have grown up as part of the majority in their country of origin.

The work of James Marcia in the 1960s and his evolving theories about how identity develops are foundational to many identity theories. In his initial theory, Marcia described identity development occurring through four statuses: foreclosure, identity diffusion, moratorium, and identity achievement (Marcia, 2002). Marcia (2002) recognized that in adults there can be an "identity reconstruction" (p. 15) process in which an experience produces disequilibrium and prompts a re-formation period that can influence one's identity. This reconstruction would not disintegrate an individual's identity; rather it would allow for a revisiting of developmental tasks to determine if current life experiences require different approaches. Marcia's (2009) recent research highlights that developmental statuses are not static and accomplished; rather a moratorium-achievement-moratorium-achievement (MAMA) reformation cycle occurs within each status.

Because identity is formed through the interactions between self and others, historical events and values set by those in the majority (others) influence identity development. These values are mainly formed by the dominant group and as Tatum (1997) explained, "The dominant group holds the power and the authority in society relative to the subordinates and determines how that power and authority may be acceptably used" (p. 23). Images of historically subordinate groups are presented as inferior to the dominant group and provide the rationale for the oppression of the subordinate group as an acceptable behavior. As a result, the subsequent cycle causes those from a minority social group to tend to embed those negative images in their organized experiences. Thus, the development of identity for someone from an oppressed group adds a more complex developmental task (Abes & Kasch, 2007; Jones & Abes, 2013; Torres et al., 2003).

Social identities, such as gender, race, ethnicity, or sexual orientation, influence who we are, how we see ourselves, and how we relate to other aspects of our lives (Jones & Abes, 2013). The social identity we are exploring, "Latino ethnic identity," is a panethnic expression that describes the experience of growing up as a Latinx minority in the United States. This social construction of minority is critical to understanding the identity development of Latinos in the United States. The increase in the Latinx population referred to in chapter 1 illustrates that the relatively young age of this population will require college and university administrators, faculty, and staff to understand the issues that influence how Latinx students make meaning of their identity.

Latino Ethnic Identity Theories

Many of the models or theories around ethnic identity tend to take on one of three frameworks. The first is social identity theory, the second is acculturation and cultural conflict, and the third is identity formation (Phinney, 1990). The social identity theories focus on membership in a particular group, like racial or ethnic groups, but may not address issues about how oppression of marginalized groups can promote potentially negative images for members of those groups (Torres, 2011). Negative images influence an individual's desire to belong to or separate from the ethnic group and seek out being accepted by the majority.

Along a different framework, the acculturation and cultural conflict frameworks tend to focus on how immigrants relate to the dominant majority culture. Recent research within this framework does attempt to explain the maintenance of ethnic identity over generations (Berry, Phinney, San, & Vedder, 2006), but even with this addition there are inherent limitations in applying this framework to the development of ethnic identity among college students. The admissions criteria that require admitted students to have English proficiency assume a certain level of acculturation among the college student population. While it is likely to look very different depending on the geographic area of the country, there tends to be some level of acculturation among Latinx students in higher education.

There are models of Latino ethnic identity that use a strong acculturation framework and therefore provide categories in which Latinos can be viewed (Félix-Ortiz de la Garza, Newcomb, & Myers, 1995; Ferdman & Gallegos, 2001; Keefe & Padilla, 1987; Torres, 1999). These theories tend to categorize Latinos by their level of acculturation to the majority culture and their pride in their ethnic culture of origin (Torres & Delgado-Romero, 2008). The categories indicate bicultural (cultural blending), Latino oriented (Latino identified), American identified (Anglo oriented), or marginal (not fitting in) (Torres & Delgado-Romero, 2008). The theories that reflect a more developmental focus on the influences Latinos experience in their ethnic identity formation focus more on processes. Ruiz (1990) conceptualized five stages from case studies in his counseling practice. The stages are causal, cognitive, consequence, working through, and successful resolution. These stages have some similarity to other racial/ethnic theories because individuals go from negative images of being Latino to a greater acceptance of self, Latino culture, and their ethnicity (Torres & Delgado, Romero, 2008).

The last framework, identity formation, is the one used in this chapter because it acknowledges the dynamic nature of ethnic identity, the influence of time or experiences, and context (Phinney, 1990). This type of identity formation framework tends to emphasize the developmental nature of identity and is most appropriate for the model presented within this chapter.

In identifying how Latino college students situate their ethnic identity, Torres (2003a; 2004a) found four conditions that influence how Latinx college students make meaning of their ethnic identity when they begin their college careers. These conditions are environment where they grew up, family and generational status in the United States, self-perception of status in society, and college environment. These conditions are interrelated and influence each other; therefore, they should be considered together rather than separately. The more dissonance between the environment in which they grew up and the college environment, the more likely cultural conflicts will play a role in their self-identification. Context is a critical element in the development of identity.

Using a framework that considers cognitive, identity, and interpersonal dimensions, Torres and Hernandez (2007) found that Latinx college students in this longitudinal study have additional developmental tasks during the college years. Perhaps the most important of these tasks is the recognition of racism and the ability to make meaning of how racism can influence their identity development. While Latinx students may understand that racism exists, it is not until individuals face racism against them (or their culture) that the reality of oppression truly influences their identity. Because some of the participants in this study grew up in areas where Latinos were the majority, they may not have experienced racism until they left their hometowns. This type of dissonance has a strong influence on how Latinx students resolve questions about their identity. This finding indicates that practitioners should also think about how to recognize racism and microaggressions in order to help Latinx students (and all students) make meaning of racism in their environment. The next section will present the framework of holistic development (often called self-authorship) and the synergy among the cognitive, identity, and interpersonal dimensions of development where the resolution of racism emerged in the data as a developmental task.

Holistic Development and Latino College Students

Kegan (1982) conceptualized the idea that three dimensions of development occur in a synergistic manner. Often referred to as *self-authorship*, it is the idea of a holistic model of development that incorporates multiple dimensions of development. Baxter Magolda's (2001) study demonstrated four phases of the journey toward self-authorship as individuals moved from external to internal self-definition. The first phase, *following external formulas*, refers to following formulas from the external world and lacking the ability to develop one's own voice. The second phase, *the crossroads*, is instigated with the dissatisfaction of following external formulas. One begins to consider one's own needs and perspectives. The third phase, *becoming the author of one's own life*, results in deciding one's own perspective and identity, and how to manage relationships with others. The fourth phase, *internal formulas*, is defined as managing external influences rather than being controlled by them. One develops interdependent relationships that take into consideration external circumstances and others' needs and honor one's own internal foundation. The central concerns (dimensions) of Baxter Magolda's participants focused on three questions: "How do I know?" (cognitive); "Who am I?" (intrapersonal); and "What relationships do I want?" (interpersonal). These questions illustrate the "intertwining of multiple dimensions of self-authorship" (Baxter Magolda, 2005, p. 87).

Torres and Baxter Magolda (2004) found linkages between ethnic identity and cognitive development. One of the findings from this longitudinal study of Latinx college students is that "ethnic identity [the intrapersonal dimension] is intricately interwoven with cognitive and interpersonal dimensions of development" (p. 343). Focusing on the effects of cognitive dissonance, Torres and Baxter Magolda found that students' cognitive development allowed them to critically evaluate negative messages and prompted reconstruction in interpersonal and intrapersonal dimensions as the students made meaning of the dissonance.

Further investigation by Torres and Hernández (2007) indicates that while Latinx college students display many of the characteristics described in Baxter Magolda's (2001) study, they also have additional developmental tasks that are not present in her research study of predominantly White students. Latinx students in the first phase, following external formulas, tended to see their family and trusted peers as their authority. Based on the level of trust, other authority figures may be seen as reliable sources of information, but it cannot be assumed that a title will automatically create trust. Students' intrapersonal (ethnic identity) dimension tended to be focused on geographic definitions (e.g., from Mexico), determined by family, or influenced by negative stereotypes. The interpersonal dimension illustrated the construct of cultural orientation (Torres, 1999). Students who were externally defined avoided anything outside of their comfort zone and tended to view culture in a dichotomous manner (e.g., either Latino or Anglo).

The students who progressed into the second phase, crossroads, recognized, and several experienced, a racist event that promoted them to question the negative images held by the society, which in turn influenced their development. These students were characterized by their ability to understand multiple perspectives that allowed them to make deliberate choices about how negative stereotypes would influence their self-perceptions. Having the cognitive skills to transform negative images about their own cultural heritage into positive images allowed them to resolve some of the cultural conflicts that come with ethnic identity. Their cognitive development prompted the ability to distinguish and choose between the positive and negative cultural choices that influence their intrapersonal dimension. In the interpersonal dimension, students began to incorporate greater diversity and manage the influences from their family in a balanced manner that did not negate the familial attachment.

In the third phase, becoming the author of one's own life, the Latinx students were able to internalize their own choices and integrate those choices into their daily lives. These cognitive and intrapersonal developmental tasks promoted an informed Latinx identity. An informed identity acknowledges the choices made between the cultures and the need to renegotiate relationships that are consistent with this evolving informed Latinx perspective. The few students who progressed into the fourth and final phase, internal foundations, were able to maintain their internalized choices and identity regardless of context. These students lived an interdependent lifestyle that maintained their own cultural values while also valuing diverse environments within their lives. Table 3.1 demonstrates the developmental tasks taken by Latinx students within the holistic framework.

The analyses of these longitudinal data also demonstrated several important considerations regarding the developmental process. For some of these students, there was fluctuation between the areas of growth that was halted or regressed due to insufficient support and, in some cases, overwhelmingly negative messages. This indicated that students who experience dissonance without support or had negative support for change tended to stagnate in their development across the dimensions. Another consideration is that students who grew up in the Latino monocultural environment and attended college within this environment had little dissonance; therefore, they did not need to resolve differences that would promote development. This is likely to be a similar phenomenon for White students who do not experience diverse environments and only know what is familiar.

These additional assumptions about development illustrate the complex nature of Latinx student development. The ability to recognize racism was a critical moment for students entering the crossroads phase. This aspect of development is consistent with other literature about ethnic identity development and the dissonance caused by racism (Cross, 1995; Phinney, 1993; Torres & Baxter Magolda, 2004).

The inclusion of ethnic identity into the holistic development model provided insight into the unique tasks Latinx students must master during their developmental process. Researchers and practitioners should

TABLE 3.1

Matrix of Holistic Development That Includes Latino Cultural Choices

Question of Interest	*Dimension*	*External Formulas*	*Crossroads*	*Becoming Author of One's Life*	*Internal Foundation*
How do I know?	Cognitive	• Family and known peers are the authority	• Expands own views to recognize multiple perspectives • Recognizes racism	• Recognizes their own cultural reality and internalizes choices between cultures to create their own principles	• Knowledge and decisions are contextually interpreted and inclusive of cultural choices
Who am I?	Intrapersonal (Ethnic Identity)	• Geographic definition of identity • Identity is determined by family. May believe negative stereotypes of Latinos	• Recognition of stereotypes and deliberate choice about how they influence self • Understanding of positive and negative cultural choices	• Integration of cultural choices into daily life—an informed Latino/a identity • Advocate for Latinos	• Comfortable illustrating culture in behavior and choices • No longer intimidated by differences
What relationships do I want with others?	Interpersonal (Cultural Orientation)	• Avoid anything outside of comfort zone • Dichotomous view of culture (either Latino or Anglo) • Negative support to try new experiences	• Change in environment (place or friends) brings about new diversity that is incorporated into social circle • Manages family influence • Ease with individuals from multiple perspectives	• Renegotiate relationships that are more consistent with an informed Latino perspective	• Living an interdependence that maintains own cultural values within the context of a diverse environment

Source: Torres, V., & Hernandez, E. (2007). The influence of ethnic identity on self-authorship: A longitudinal study of Latino/a college students. *Journal of College Student Development, 48*(5), pp. 558–573. Reprinted with permission from ACPA College Student Educators International.

consider this recognition of racism as part of the process of development. More importantly, the process of reconstructing negative images as positive images is facilitated by support from mentors within the students' environment. It is important to recognize that externally defined Latinx students seek support from known sources such as family and friends, instead of traditional higher education authority figures, like advisers or faculty. Support services professionals cannot assume that a title will garner trust. Instead, they must recognize the need to establish a relationship with Latinx students in order for them to be seen as sources of information and viewed as trusted authority figures. This support is where institutions can make a difference for Latinx students' development.

A New Latino Ethnic Identity Model for the College and Adult Years

The lifespan model uses data from these studies to provide a synthesis of findings that looks across the lifespan of Latinx college students and adults. The nature of a synthesis model is to pull together what is learned from multiple studies and illustrate the findings in a different, more complete manner. By considering all the findings among the studies, we can better describe the development of Latino identity through statuses and transitions. The transitions explain the change process that occurred among these individuals. The transitions from one status to the next are characterized by reflection about the individual's experience with their context; therefore, we are calling these *borderlands experiences*. This phrase comes from the work of Gloria Anzaldúa (1987) and references the place between two cultures. This phrase is used because although these can be transitions, they also serve as places to explore issues between the cultures without necessarily committing to cultural behaviors and internal beliefs. The model is presented in two parts; the complete model is provided at the end. Using examples of the data, each phase will be described. Figure 3.1 provides the first two statuses and the elements that influence transitions.

Defining Self Externally

Externally defined students focus on how others have defined their ethnicity for them (Torres, 2003a). Three conditions tend to emerge within this status and provide the contextual nature of these externally defined ideas of identity: focus on geographic location, extent of diversity in community, and parents' perception of ethnicity.

In his first year of college, Bob described the meaning of being Hispanic as: "Hispanic because I was born in the United States, and Mexican because

Figure 3.1. Lifespan model of Latinx identity development, part 1.

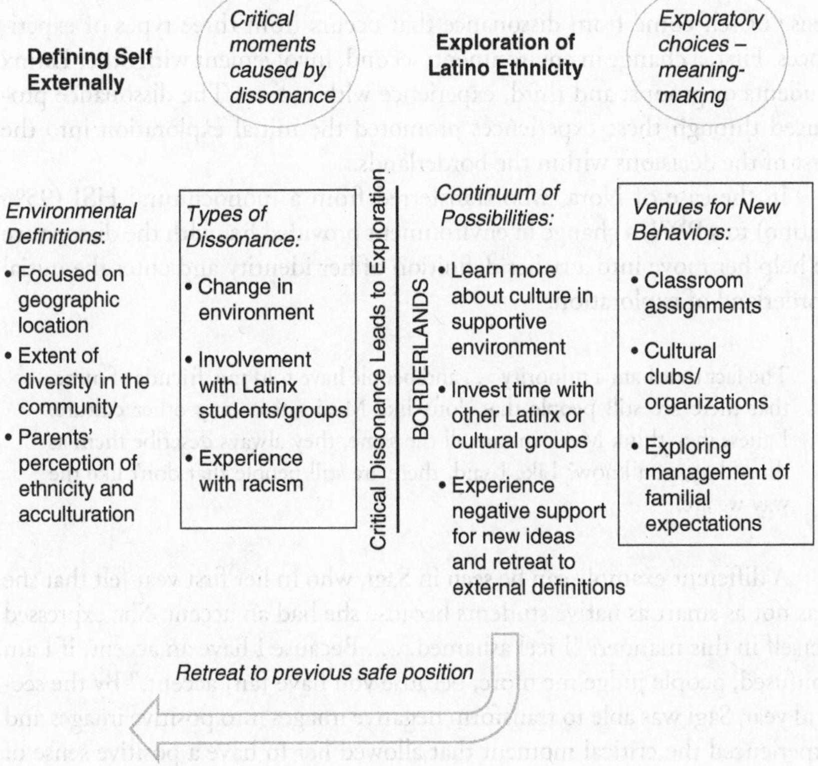

. . . everybody in my family is Mexican." Bob's focus was on his family's geographic origin and where he currently lived. It was in many ways a statement of fact, not a cultural understanding of his life.

The second condition, the extent of diversity in the community, describes individuals who took their diversity for granted because everyone was like them or those who had to explain themselves to others. In the case of Carlos, he was from an area that was over 90% Latino, but he attended a PWI. In his first year, he described his experiences as a Latino in this manner: "Before, when I was at home, everybody knew I was Hispanic. . . . Everybody knows I am Mexican . . . [and] 90% of the students [in my high school] were of Hispanic background. Now I come and I have to say my name differently . . . I have to educate people about who I am" (Torres, 2003a, p. 53).

The final contextual condition is focused on parents' perceptions. When asked if being Puerto Rican meant anything to Jebus, he said, "It is just like—really I don't know what it would mean. It is just I have been told throughout my life I am Puerto Rican, so that is what I say."

Transition: Critical Moments Caused by Dissonance

The change behaviors that can move an individual out of externally defined sense of self come from dissonance that occurs from three types of experiences. First, a change in environment; second, involvement with other Latinx students or groups; and third, experience with racism. The dissonance produced through these experiences promoted the initial exploration into the first of the decisions within the borderlands.

In the case of Nora, who transferred from a monocultural HSI (95% Latino) to a PWI, a change in environment provided her with the dissonance to help her move into a richer definition of her identity and enter the initial borderland of exploration.

> The fact that I am a minority . . . and people have told me, friends of mine, that there are still people that don't like Mexicans or any other culture. I guess they think Mexicans are all the same, they always describe them as short, lazy, you know? Like I said, there are still people that don't like the way we are.

A different example can be seen in Sagi, who in her first year felt that she was not as smart as native students because she had an accent. She expressed herself in this manner: "I feel ashamed. . . . Because I have an accent, if I am confused, people judge me more, because you have [an] accent." By the second year, Sagi was able to transform negative images into positive images and experienced the critical moment that allowed her to have a positive sense of self. She described it in this manner: "I feel like I want to show them that I can do the job, even though I have an accent, I am able to be understood to other people, Americans, and I am trying. I am trying."

These conditions allowed for change only when some sort of dissonance created a borderland incident for the individuals to resolve. These incidents allowed them to question their externally defined understanding of ethnicity and deepen their understanding of self within the context of the two cultures. Individuals who experienced support through change behaviors prompted by dissonance moved into the next status: exploration of ethnicity.

Exploration of Latinx Ethnicity

As individuals emerged from the borderlands with a desire to have greater understanding of their Latinx ethnicity, they explored their identity through a continuum of possibilities. This continuum can include learning about culture in a supportive environment or investing time with other Latinos or cultural groups. The majority of participants in this status had positive experiences during exploration. It should be noted that if the exploration becomes a negative experience, and the individual does not have sufficient support for new ideas and behaviors, then retreat to the previously defined external self is possible. This retreat provides a safer position for the individual by allowing them to maintain previously held beliefs about their ethnicity and the surrounding context.

Individuals can approach this exploration phase with great enthusiasm or with hesistance, as if they were checking the temperature of the water. There is a set of cognitive skills that must also be developed during this exploration. The Latinx individual must be able to evaluate information about Latinos (negative images or racist ideology) to truly make meaning of how these images apply. It should be understood that oppression may feel heaviest in this status. It is critical to recognize that negative support for experiences in this status can promote retreat and reinforce negative images or racist ideology.

In her second year, Maggie said this about how she self-defined: "I think it has changed for the stronger. . . . Now I actually do embrace my ethnicity a lot more than I did last year. And I'm proud to be a Mexican American, or you would like to say a 'Hispanic.'"

When asked how this change came about she shared:

> Our youth, from church, went to Georgia and Alabama and gave a concert and I speak English pretty fluently, so I went into this store and I met up with this person that just kept looking at me and I felt kind of uncomfortable. . . . And this person just kept on following me around and didn't think that I spoke English and he's like "Oh these darn Mexicans, they just come over here and take our stuff," and I'm like, that just freaked me out.

Upon returning to the campus, Maggie talked to her peers about the incident, and they supported her understanding of this experience as racist and what it meant for her to experience racism for the first time. Had she not been able to process and receive positive support for understanding racism, she may have regressed back into external definitions and been vulnerable to stereotype threat. She said, "When I became more involved in the school that's when I embraced who I am. And I just really don't care about what people think about me anymore. I mean, it does hurt." The support received from her peers and later a mentor allowed Maggie the space and time to reflect and make meaning of her experiences. Without this level of support for reflection the meaning-making process may not have occurred.

It should be noted that the individuals who experienced incidents of racism while participating in this study often spoke about initially not wanting to share the incidents with others. Again, the trusted others were able to create an atmosphere to allow them to share these painful experiences and make meaning of the negative images prevalent in society.

Another individual exploring his ethnicity was Juan, who, in his fourth year of college, talked about how he was using his classroom assignments to learn about his own heritage.

> I guess sometimes the best way to learn your own culture is just try to discover it yourself. And I was like—so . . . that is why I decided to, like a bunch of my school projects since then have been somewhat Latino oriented. Probably because it is fun to learn, and see what else I can learn about the culture. Like I have a . . . paper and I decided to do it on the temple of Tenochtitlan, the Aztec temple.

Juan slowly explored his Latino identity through classroom assignments. The ability to research aspects of his identity allowed him to reframe the beliefs he had as a first-year student. Namely, he imagined Latinos living in the bad part of town, but his parents were economically better off and could live in the good part of town. While Juan never referred back to those beliefs, his self-image as a Mexican American was changed as a result of being able to research positive role models and the accomplishments of his ancestors.

A few students had an experience that supported negative images and as a result they retreated to previously held external definitions. One example was Alejandra, who began her college years in an education cohort. In her second year, she had an experience with an Anglo member of her cohort regarding her slight accent. Alejandra described her experience by saying, "Then this girl in the cohort, she is White, and she [said] like you have grammar problems. . . . She was like you have poor grammar, but this is okay because you weren't born here, or something like that."

Although Alejandra was born in the United States, she internalized the negative view of the very slight accent she had as a result of growing up speaking Spanish at home. When asked how she reacted to this exchange with the other student, she responded by saying:

> Maybe she didn't care when she said it. She wasn't thinking. But I took it personally because, I don't know. That is an issue I have with myself. . . . Every time I talk, it is in my mind: "You have poor grammar."

This negative experience caused Alejandra to retreat to a previous external definition of herself regarding her inability to speak in the manner her peers considered proper English. Although she was born in the United States, the fact that she was bilingual made her feel deficient rather than proficient in two languages, a skill other students did not have. Though she later overcame this negative incident, this experience stalled her development, and it was years before she made meaning of this as a negative message that she did not need to internalize.

Transition: Exploring Choices and Meaning-Making

The behaviors used by individuals to explore their ethnicity focused on a variety of contexts, but most prevalent were classroom assignments, cultural clubs/organizations, or management of familial expectations. In the previous section, Juan talked about using a paper from a history course "to see what else I can learn about the culture." Maggie used the support from peers within a student organization to help her make meaning of the racist behavior she encountered when she left her monocultural Latino environment and visited a predominantly White area of the country. It was the exploration of managing familial expectations that was at times the most difficult for some students. In this transition, students needed to engage in exploration and make meaning of the familial expectations that are common within the Latino culture. The meaning-making process determined if these new beliefs and behaviors were retained as part of their identity. Without integrating these new beliefs, individuals can remain in this neutral space of exploration without committing to having their ethnicity be part of their identity. To illustrate this transition, we use an example of a student struggling to manage familial expectations.

Rosalie often commented on the strictness of her parents. She referenced this as traditional Latinx parental behaviors grounded in the cultural values from her country of origin, Mexico. As she began to manage the relationship with her mother, she described the interaction in this manner: "And with my mom, I just tell her, you know I know her [mother's] obsessions, but 'this is what's happening, this is what's going on, this is how it's going to be,' we just work things out like that." In this case, Rosalie began to talk to her mother and explain what she had to do rather than accept that she had limitations that emerged from her cultural heritage that were rigid and not open to negotiation or management. This task was particularly difficult for the women in this study but also affected the men when they attempted to do something that was not seen as part of the norm within their culture.

The remaining status in the model, committed Latino identity, requires students to once again enter into the borderlands to practice the continuous meaning-making that occurs in adult life. Every new situation or environment can prompt a meaning-making reflection about how we fit in or how we will be interpreted. Figure 3.2 illustrates the final status within the lifespan model.

Figure 3.2. Lifespan model of Latinx identity development, part 2.

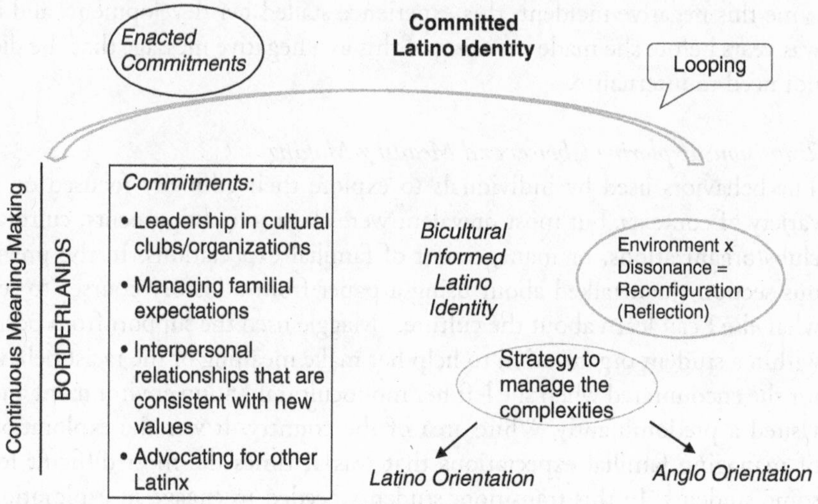

Students who successfully made meaning of their new beliefs and experiences during their exploratory choice entered another borderlands characterized by continuous meaning-making. This borderland transition incorporates higher levels of cognitive skills where ideas are constantly evaluated regarding their understanding self within new contexts. Because of the greater complexity gained as part of the continuing cognitive development, there was no evidence of individuals returning to externally defined definitions from this point on in the model. This point is also where Latinx individuals returned when a major life change prompted an evaluation of how they fit in or were perceived in the new context. This continuous meaning-making was further enhanced in the next phase through commitment behaviors. At this point, the transition between exploring behaviors and commitment behaviors were nuanced and distinguished only through the idea of more complex meaning-making.

Transition: Enacted Commitments

As the continuous meaning-making process becomes a natural part of reflection within the borderlands, Latinx individuals became much more comfortable with their sense of self and being "Latino." The commitments that emerged in this transition were seen through leadership in cultural clubs/ organizations, managing familial expectations, interpersonal relationships that are consistent with new values, and advocating for other Latinx.

In the case of Maria, she began her studies at a community college within her hometown and then transferred to a university away from home. She described her peer group after she transferred as the following:

> I definitely feel really comfortable with Dominicans who don't feel like they're American at all, and I definitely feel less comfortable with Americans who have no connection with their ethnic background or anything like that. But I definitely understand that I'm definitely American, like I know that.

In this statement, Maria acknowledged the borderland that exists for all of us who interact among multiple cultures. She may prefer her close friends to be Dominican but clearly acknowledged that she balances this with her Americanized cultural identity. This understanding did not come to Maria until her fourth year of college after she changed her environment by transferring to the university away from her hometown. The change in context required her to access a new set of beliefs and behaviors in order to understand herself within the new environment.

Committed Latino Identity

Again, it is important to acknowledge that this status begins by recognizing that continuous meaning-making processes are occurring and the individual must embrace them as a common part of daily existence. In this status, the borderland process comes first because it is in these borderlands that the person commits to an informed Latino identity (Torres & Hernandez, 2007) that incorporates aspects of cultures in daily life. For most of the participants, the cultures were Latino and U.S. cultures. The commitment behaviors may be tested when a change in context occurs, but it is only when these committed behaviors become the norm that the person exhibits the internalized committed Latino identity. After much deliberation, we chose the term *bicultural informed Latino identity* to exemplify the ideals of an internalized identity that incorporates both cultures found in the borderland. We acknowledge that individuals who prefer a Latino or Anglo orientation can also have an internalized identity, but feel that these expressions of identity support a strategy to manage the complexities encountered within the borderlands. The idea that a bicultural or integrated identity, as Berry and colleagues (2006) call it, best resembles an informed Latino identity is because the reality of both cultures is ever present and constantly functioning throughout the United States. As a result, Latinos are required to simultaneously engage with both cultures.

Antonio, the undocumented valedictorian of his high school, volunteered with a local organization benefiting immigrants in the city where he lived.

He spoke to civic groups and volunteered at his former high school and for a Teen Reach program as a soccer coach. In his third year, Antonio talked about the importance of doing this work and illustrated his own enacted commitments that informed his Latino identity.

> Among the most important things I think is happening, well it's about to happen right now, again there's a Dream Act which is a Senate bill that will help . . . [un]documented students receive some kind of legal residency . . . . But what I am really doing right now is trying to educate the people that don't know about the [Dream Act] and the ones that already know about [it], try to tell them that we need their help again to get this bill passed.

Few students had internalized committed identities. One of the few was Elizabeth who had previously struggled with her Spanish last name and not speaking the language. Her reaction when she returned from being abroad illustrates her recognition and committed bicultural informed identity in her fourth-year interview.

> They [people in her study abroad country] are so much different, before when [I] don't speak with them and you don't really know what kind of culture that is, and like how to react. I started to realize that I had that culture in me, I just didn't know that it was a culture. And I noticed in South America, people were like "This is tradition," and I am like, oh yeah, we do this all the time [at home]. And I didn't really realize that it was different from the American style tradition. . . . And when I got back, and we started speaking in Spanish, it wasn't a big deal for me, and I was just like, oh whatever, and he [Cuban friend] was like why didn't we do this before? And I was like oh, yeah there is a big reason for that [she did not recognize she had culture around her].

Because identity is socially constructed and constantly interacting with the context or environment, it is important to acknowledge that once a person achieves an internalized identity, it does not mean that they will never go through a meaning-making process again. For this reason, a research team surveyed adult Latinos and found a process we termed *looping* (Torres, Martinez, Wallace, Medrano, Robledo, & Hernandez, 2012).

Transition: Looping

Looping emerged as a process where individuals loop back to a previous point in their development and reevaluate how their socially constructed identity may need to be adapted as a result of being in a different environment or different life event. We began to see this reevaluation as a looping process that brought individuals to question aspects of their identity that they had previously configured. Yet this looping process seemed to indicate a more complex understanding of self; therefore, the looping did not entail a complete questioning of identity, but rather a refinement of how Latino identity was considered within the context of changes in their lives. The term *looping* was selected to illustrate how this process of reevaluating Latino identity can be cyclical in nature and is likely to happen repeatedly throughout adult life as changes in context and lifestyle occur.

Among the participants in the study of adult Latinos, 35% of the respondents revisited issues of identity during adulthood. In all cases, it should be noted that this revisiting took them back to redefining their continuous meaning-making borderland and that their internalized identity was influenced but not necessarily discarded. The results of this study indicated that two themes tended to describe the prompting of reevaluation of identity (looping process) among the participants. The first theme was the influence of the environment on identity. This influence was most often focused on managing the environmental changes and how their identity was viewed differently within different contexts.

The second theme was life circumstances that caused major changes in an individual's identity, such as a job relocation, a marriage, or another major life event that prompted an assessment of one's sense of self. Gilbert's initial questioning of his identity was described when he reflected back to high school:

> I heard derogatory comments from fellow classmates regarding the actions of *cholos* [a Mexican American who is involved in a countercultural group or gang] in our schools. I wanted these students, other students, faculty, and staff to know that the actions of a few isolated individuals [do] not characterize all persons who share the same ethnic background.

Later he described a major life circumstance that prompted a reevaluation of his identity. In this example, the life circumstances caused an assessment of identity and started the looping process that initated continuous meaning-making about how one commits to identity.

> As an adult I was victimized in a home invasion robbery, during which the 2 criminals attempted to sever my spinal cord. My physical and mental recovery process took approximately 12 months, and during that time I questioned many things including my identity. In the end I emerged with a stronger sense of self and a renewed commitment to seeking to facilitate personal, community, organizational, and societal change on a daily basis.

Gilbert's story expresses how he refined his sense of self with a greater commitment to an internalized identity.

Another example is from Cella, a 51-year-old woman who initially described her identity as "I didn't fit in any of their stereotypes of a Mexican." Later she explained how environmental changes or life changes required that she think about her identity differently.

> The only thing I can think of is when I got married. I had to learn how to fully embrace another culture (African American) in my home life, especially as it impacted our children. My husband and I both had to learn how to hold onto our cultural uniqueness while also validating each other's cultural heritage.

During the participants' looping processes, none of them returned to earlier externally defined ideas of identity. Instead the individuals who experienced looping returned to the borderlands' continuous meaning-making that becomes a daily part of a committed Latino identity. In Figure 3.3 we present the model as a whole to provide a complete picture of how the lifespan model interconnects with the status and transitions.

Summary

The lifespan Latinx identity development model illustrates that identity is not static, but rather constantly being evaluated. The idea of looping is consistent with Marcia's (2002) ideas about reevaluation of identity that occurs among adults but incorporates the concept of borderlands as a different developmental transition that occurs for those of us who manage two cultures within our daily lives. The remaining chapters will expand on other aspects of the ways in which the environment and other factors can influence how individuals develop their sense of self.

Figure 3.3 Lifespan model of Latinx identity development.

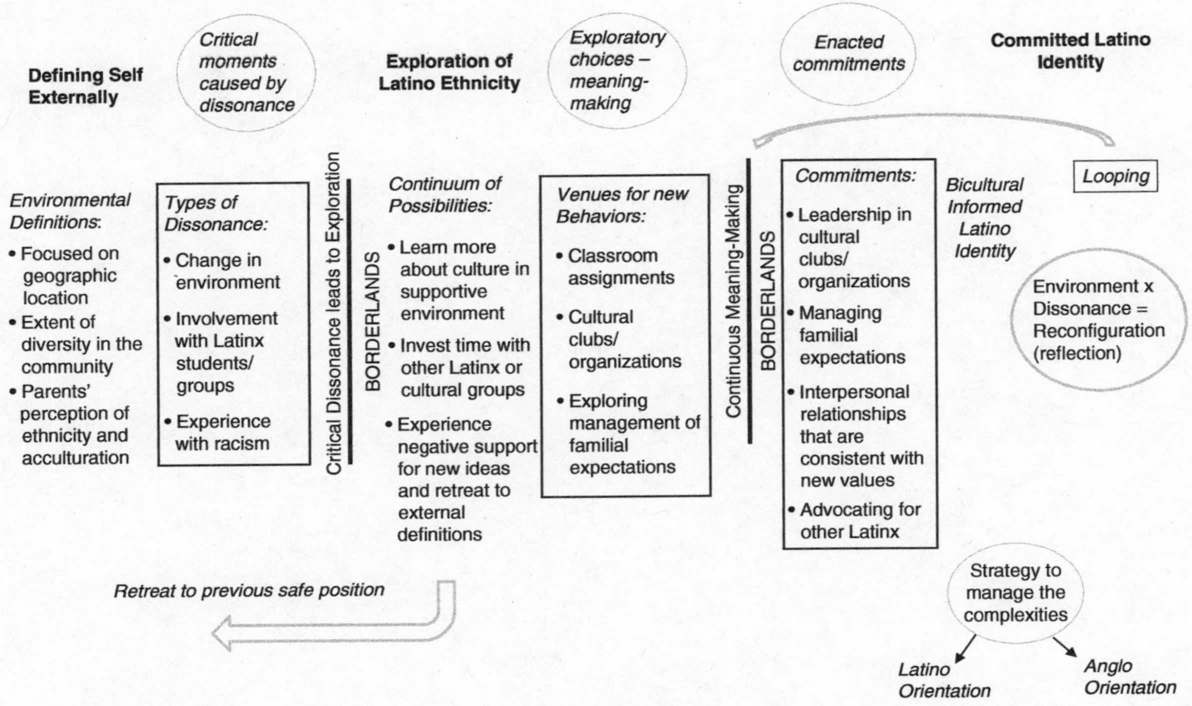

4

ENVIRONMENTAL INFLUENCES ON THE EXPERIENCES OF LATINX INDIVIDUALS

In many ways, the difficulty understanding the experiences of individuals encompassed under the panethnic term *Latinx* is encompassed by the realization that each person can make different choices based on individual context. In this chapter, the various environmental contexts that can influence the experiences of Latinx college students and adults are explored. The data used to explore these issues are both qualitative and quantitative and were collected during the longitudinal study of Latinx college students and the Latinx adults study. Chapter 5 will dive deeper into aspects of intersecting identities and context.

In these studies, we considered multiple types of environmental contexts that may influence the experiences of Latinx individuals. This chapter focuses on environmental influences by looking at three aspects. The first type is the campus environment, which includes the structural diversity of the campus as well as the community in which the institution is based. The second type is the connections within the institutional environment that support students. The third type of contextual environment encompasses societal factors like family, peers, and social constructions of how Latinos are seen within the U.S. context. The last section of this chapter includes a discussion of how these environmental contexts can create cultural conflicts for the individual and an exploration of what this conflict encompasses.

Environmental Influences

Because we were interested in the influence of identity on participants' experiences, we began with understanding the role of context (environmental and other variables) on developing a sense of self. The research on identity development has always included how identity is situated within the larger context that the individual navigates (Jones & Abes, 2013). Individuals develop identity as they organize experiences that occur in everyday life within the context of the environment (Erickson, 1994). Although this interplay between environment and identity is generally accepted, identity theories that explain the organization of identity may only mention the environmental influences and not elaborate on the differences, or nondifferences, that result within various contexts. The role of environmental influences is most often cited in higher education within the context of environmental fit between the college student and the campus environment to understand its contribution to integration and retention (Tinto, 1993). In the following section we will explore the perceptions of college environments and the influence environments can have on the experiences of Latinx college students and in some cases adult Latinos.

Campus Environments

Students' perceptions of the college environment can serve as "a potential determinant of future interactions and outcomes" (Hurtado, Milem, Clayton-Pedersen, & Allen, 1999, p. 25). There is a fairly consistent understanding that experience with diversity has positive outcomes for students (Bowman, 2011). These positive outcomes are greater for White students (Bowman, 2012), yet visible diversity does provide comfort for underrepresented students. The racial tension, or discrimination, is more critical for Latinx students whose educational aspirations can be influenced by negative perceptions within the college environment (Hurtado, Carter, & Spuler, 1996; Suarez-Balcazar, Orellana-Damacela, Portillo, Rowan, & Andrews-Guillen, 2003). In order to explore these issues, it is important to consider aspects of the model presented in chapter 3, as well as what is known about the campus environment and its influence on students.

Studies that consider Latinx students' perceptions of the college environment illustrate the inconclusive understanding of its effect on Latinx student experiences. The limited number of research studies looking at Latinx college students is further limited by the lack of variety among institutional environments. As previously stated, Latinx students at PWIs are expected to assimilate into the campus environment (culture) (Gloria & Castellanos, 2003), but there is less information about what happens to students in other institutional types. Gloria (1997) compared two university environments, one being predominantly White and another described as diverse. This study found that for all students the university environment was the strongest predictor for explaining the variance of nonpersistence decisions, and friend support was the next highest predictor of retention at both types of institutions. While the magnitude of influence varied between the two environments, the same predictors emerged for both types of institutions (Gloria, 1997).

The creation of HSIs created a different environment to consider. The HSI designation is primarily due to the geographic proximity of these institutions to areas with large numbers of Latinx students (Gasman, 2008; Laden, 2001). While HSIs represent approximately 12% of colleges and universities in the United States, they enroll approximately 60% of Latinx students in higher education (Santiago et al., 2016). Much of the attention on HSIs is oriented toward structure, policy, and funding arenas, and less research is devoted to the experiences of students at these institutions.

Some researchers see HSIs as positive influences on access for Latinx students, (Contreras, Malcom, & Bensimon, 2008; Cuellar, 2015; de los Santos & de los Santos, 2003) while others see these institutions as reinforcing some of the cultural challenges Latinx students face in higher education (Dayton, Gonzalez-Vasquez, Martinez, & Plum, 2004). Because most students attending HSIs live at home "students remain in an environment where the cultural values concerning family responsibility are continually reinforced, [and] academic responsibilities and regular progress may be compromised" (Dayton et al., 2004, p. 33). The following sections examine the environmental perceptions of Latinx college students within three types of college environments and consider how changes in the environment may influence identity and other factors important to the experiences of Latinx students.

Perceptions of Environments

To describe the various perceptions of the campus environment, the data are presented by institutional type. Students who attended the PWI noticed the lack of diversity in the college environment and tried to seek out other Latinos. In her first year, Lulu described her urban university as more diverse than the other state-funded institutions, but she perceived it as what she termed *fake diversity*.

> I felt like it was more diverse [than] other colleges that are isolated in the countryside. It is kind of like a fake diversity, because how can you have diversity when it is just the majority of the student are Caucasian.

This quote reveals the subjective perception of how *diversity* is defined on college campuses. Though Lulu selected her institution because it was the most diverse campus in the state, she does not perceive that diversity really existed within the university. Araceli, who attended the same PWI as Lulu, agreed that the demographics of the institution were diverse, but she articulated frustration in actually seeing this diversity. In a first-year interview, she described how she perceived the diversity in the environment.

> I think there is [*sic*] a lot of Latinos. . . . But they don't tend to branch out and meet other Latinos. [Here] you are walking to class, and you look straight, and you don't talk to anyone—it is not friendly. So I was like, okay where did everyone go? And they say that 10% of the school is Latino, but you don't see them. It is kind of, where are they at? They are hiding? And I know for me the Latinos that I know it is because of MECHA [student organization for Latino students].

Both of these examples illustrate differences between how the individuals perceive the diversity within its student body and Latinx students within the same institution might perceive the diversity. The Latinx students in this study appreciated the fact that among the state institutions this urban university was the most diverse but continued to feel that there was not much diversity on campus. How students define *diversity* is dependent on their own contextual experiences and thus influences how they perceive the environment.

The perceptions were more varied among the students at the diverse HSI. Antonio found the university a welcoming environment because he perceived there were many Latinos. In his first-year interview, he stated,

> Well, the things that I found that are good for me is that we have a lot of Hispanic students, so as I said, I feel very comfortable around Latinos, so that is one of the good things at the university.

The perception of the same institutional environment was different for Veronica who felt she had to be careful with whom she spoke because she feared feeling unwelcome. She described her perception in her first-year interview, saying

> I kind of feel different. Sometimes I feel like I have my eyes open, I'll be more quiet, you know, and I'll be more observant than most people and see who is more acceptable to talk to.

Laura perceived less belongingness because she looked different and did not see as much diversity as she expected at this HSI. She described her perceptions in her first-year interview.

> Actually, it is a little different because sometimes when you are in your Hispanic or Mexican community, you feel more at home and when you are

here [at the university], you feel more like 'do I belong here?' A little lost. Like people look down at you.

These students fluctuated between seeing diversity within their university and continuing to question if they fit into this environment. The findings among the students at the diverse HSI demonstrate the complexity of environmental perceptions and how these perceptions are linked to the level of dissonance felt from their home environment. These perceptions can influence adjustment to college. Overall, students described the university environment as containing both support and challenges, which in turn should promote the success of all students.

Participants who attended the monocultural HSI (95% Latino) were the most likely to feel comfortable in the environment. Isis described her adjustment to college in her first-year interview as "I guess it [university environment] is the same since I have lived my whole life here, I see the same people." This level of comfort did not provide exposure to differences in race and ethnicity and thus some of the students were uncomfortable leaving the safe environment. Carla talked about the environment in her first-year interview by saying:

> And over here everyone, I don't know I guess I feel more protected here because I have grown up with like Mexican Americans, and it is hard to for me to go somewhere else where it is just White people or Black people, and hardly any Mexican Americans. So it is just we are not really exposed to other cultures that are around.

Jennifer also talked in her first-year interview about her discomfort being around non-Latinos by saying:

> I can't say I am comfortable hanging out with Anglos because I never have. And if I have, it is just one person, or two, but then again, like they are what I call mix, or mutts. They are like half White, half Hispanic, so they don't see themselves as White. They see themselves as Hispanics, since everyone else is Hispanic. So I really . . . only hang out with Hispanics.

The students in the monocultural environment had little dissonance with the environment and campus culture; therefore, they did not have the opportunity to experience discomfort or resolve any issues that could rise from the dissonance. In some cases, the participants were actively avoiding exposure to other cultures or other ways of doing things. While this type of institutional fit is highly desirable when considering college choice models and retention (Tinto, 1993), this level of complete fit does not necessarily promote the questioning of previous ideas and may not promote student development toward more complex understanding of the self or the environment. Working through dissonance within the college environment is a desired developmental strategy for college students to develop more complex ways of thinking. Without this dissonance, these students need to experience differing perspectives in other ways, like classroom assignments, to develop into complex thinkers who can work through diverse perspectives.

Influence of Changes in the Environment

Changes in environment can take on many forms. Among the six students who transferred to a different institution, and therefore a different environment during the college years, several changes were observed.

Maria began college at an HSI (community college) and transferred in her third year to an urban PWI with a fairly diverse student body, but not an HSI. Though she thought she would never leave her hometown, after transferring she stated, "Now I can see myself [leaving], I'm even thinking about going to other countries." Maria talked about her new college environment as broadening her horizons by saying "As I go and take these courses, and I go to these different events, I am sure I wouldn't have been able to do [these things] back home. I've just seen so much in the past year." While her family was a bit "insulted" by her desire to be away from home and experience new things, they supported the change in environment and Maria's decision to leave home. When asked about her cultural orientation since she left the comforts of her hometown, Maria responded by saying:

> I think I am definitely more comfortable. . . . Before I came here, it was more segregated. In [hometown] there was [*sic*] more Hispanics, in the stores there were more Anglos, or White, if you want to say, it just felt more segregated when you walk through [the stores], so you really felt more uncomfortable. So here, especially in my dorm, I've made friends with those particular people, or people like that [Anglos], if it was for studying. Just seeing that I could actually be friends with them, it's great. It's really, really good, in that aspect. I never saw myself doing that. It was just so separated. But here, it's good experience. I definitely see myself being comfortable around all of them.

In these quotes Maria illustrated the need to have some dissonance in the environment in order to explore and thus make meaning of your own identity in the context of others. Prior to transferring, Maria could not imagine herself anywhere other than her hometown. After transferring, she could see how changes in the environment can teach new things and provide experiences that enrich one's sense of self. These changes provided her with a stronger understanding of difference and thus a stronger understanding of what it means to be part of two different cultures. In her hometown, she thought she had contact with and felt comfortable with Anglos. Yet after exposure to an unfamiliar environment, she recognized that there was segregation, and her comfort level was perhaps based on the lack of interaction, rather than real experiences. The ability to be friends with Anglos in her new environment required a certain level of maturity for Maria since this was not seen as a possibility in her hometown.

Maria's experiences with diversity in this PWI were mostly positive and she felt supported by her family and the peers she met at her new institution. This support is critical and not always found in different environments.

For Nora who transferred from a monocultural HSI environment to a PWI in her third year of college, the experience was slightly different. When asked to explain her statement "I got used to it," Nora talked about her adjustment to being a minority in her new environment.

> At the beginning, I guess, I was kind of weird [*sic*] out by the fact that the Hispanics here, or at least the ones I saw working in places, were basically just like the cooks. So that was pretty bad. It made me feel worse, because those were the people that were working here [on campus], or the janitors who were Mexican. So that was pretty hard. You try to talk to them, but, at the same time you're kind of like—one would talk to me because you're a minority here, and then you see your culture or your race being the worse [*sic*] paid, so that is pretty hard.

Being away from her Latino monocultural environment required that Nora recognize that in other environments she was perceived as a minority. Previously she had Latino role models in senior administrative positions at her urban HSI and in powerful community government positions. At her new PWI, the Latino faces she saw represented only one socioeconomic level–low paying and nonprofessional. With time she "got used to it" and was able to make meaning and learn from her experiences.

> At the beginning I wasn't comfortable with it at all, like I said it was just a huge impact of difference. But now, I can appreciate it more, because there's a lot of people who keep asking me, "Oh so you speak Spanish fluently?" and like "Yes," so that's a big deal for them that you can actually speak two languages pretty well. . . . I guess I'm becoming prouder and appreciating it more, the whole thing about being Mexican, because we're close to family. So all that I'm appreciating it more.

Though difficult, Nora understood that she had grown from being exposed to a form of diversity within her new environment, and what would be nondiverse for others. The PWI had a small percentage of students of color, and although this is a different type of monocultural environment, it provided the dissonance Nora needed to consider other perspectives and refine her sense of self and ethnic identity. The differences between the perceptions of her hometown and her new environment provided the necessary dissonance to create a developmental moment. Her ability to transform the negative images into positive ones indicated a level of cognitive sophistication that allowed her to accept that there were multiple interpretations for what she experienced and that in different contexts the roles of Latinos within the college campus were differently perceived.

Comparing the Influence of Institutional Type on Latinx College Students

The data from student stories point out that lack of dissonance between the person and the environment may not promote the level of development necessary for more complex understandings of self and others to emerge. While person–environment fit has its positive points, this study indicated that a perfect fit may not be as desirable as once thought. Today "students' intercultural skills . . . require not just knowing more facts or having more awareness, but a genuine maturity, an individual transformation that enables students to apply their knowledge and skills in a variety of contexts" (King & Baxter Magolda, 2005, p. 586). This level of intercultural maturity is difficult to achieve without exposure to difference or other dissonance that could prompt questioning within a person's ways of knowing. While not part of this research, it is reasonable to consider that the similar lack of dissonance for White students within PWIs would also hinder their ability to understand more complex ways of understanding self and others. It is unreasonable to require dissonance in the environment; therefore, the next section explores ways that monocultural campuses can promote development.

In monocultural environments, such as many PWIs and some HSIs, other forms of dissonance can help students develop their sense of self as well as their understanding of ethnicity. Coursework can challenge the students' status quo and prompt students to make meaning of different perspectives. In addition, several students traveled with church groups or family and experienced dissonance because of those temporary changes in environment. Campus administrators and faculty should consider intentional mechanisms to expose students to differences and find ways for the campus environment to promote questioning of previous ways of knowing to develop more complex understandings of the world in which we function. Without a more complex understanding of the environment, the balance and intersections between developing identity and understanding environment is not complete.

While some aspects of this study reinforce Dayton and colleagues' (2004) assertion that students at HSIs living at home may have their progression compromised, the study also highlights that not all HSIs are the same. While the students in the monocultural environment might accurately reflect this claim, some were able to experience dissonance and advance their skills while resolving differences. The students at the diverse HSI experienced sufficient dissonance to be repeatedly placed in situations that required more complex understanding of different perspectives.

These data seem to reinforce the assertion that diversity assists students in developing more complex understandings of the world. While much of this work is grounded in the need to have diverse students at PWIs (Gurin, Dey, Hurtado, & Gurin, 2002), the present study indicates that any monocultural environment should work toward ensuring diverse perspectives in their institutions. In this study the monocultural environment was predominantly Latino rather than White, yet it was the lack of diversity that became the critical difference when these students changed environments. The environmental change allowed the students to consider multiple perspectives.

The required energy to make meaning of dissonance can promote development or it can promote retreat into safer environments, as was seen for some students in the exploration of Latino ethnicity status (Torres & Hernandez, 2007). While the examples shared here indicated some development as a result of change in environment, this study included participants who received negative support for changing environments and therefore struggled to go beyond external definitions of self (Torres & Hernandez, 2007). For campus administrators the challenge is to create environments where support is matched with sufficient challenge (dissonance) to promote more complex understandings of self and others.

The majority of the students in this longitudinal study were first generation in college and often lived at home. The environmental factors that pull students away from their academic journey require that institutions pay more attention to these students (Núñez, Crisp, & Elizondo, 2015). The students in this study often spoke about needing information and advising from their institutions in order to navigate the campus environment. In this section, we look at the results of the survey data to consider environmental influences. It should be noted that the uneven sample size between the environments is a major limitation within this type of comparison analysis, yet the results provide some interesting discussion points.

The survey used in the longitudinal study consisted of previously validated scales and measures that included several personal and environmental factors. The personal factors measured were level of ethnic identity using the Multigroup Ethnic Identity Measure (MEIM) (Phinney, 1992) and level of acculturation using Short Acculturation Scale for Hispanics (Marin, Sabogal, Marin, Otero-Sabogal, & Perez-Stable, 1987). The reliability estimates for each of the scales reflected strong psychometric properties. The MEIM consists of 14 items that provide an indicator of ethnic identification with an overall reliability at an alpha coefficient of .90, and validity was obtained through factor analysis (Phinney, 1992). The acculturation scale consists of 12 items. Reliability for the total scale is an alpha coefficient of .92, and validity was attained through correlations with familial generation in the United States, time in the United States, and participants' self-evaluation of acculturation (Marin et al., 1987).

The environmental factors included items that were previously used by Nora, Kraemer, and Itzen (1997) on a group of commuter Latino community college students. Nora and colleagues' (1997) scales have been used with commuter populations in previous research studies with the following levels of reliability: family responsibilities (a = .82), encouragement (a = .78), cultural affinity (a = .77), satisfaction with faculty (a = .72), academic difficulty (a = .68), academic integration (a = .69), and institutional commitment (a = .89).

To compare the environments within each of the institutions, factorial ANOVAs with two independent variables were used. Consideration of the independent variables was determined with the goal to compare institutional environments and first-generation-in-college status. The mother's level of education was used as a determinant for first-generation-in-college status, as most of the students participating in the interviews spoke of their mother as the parent who most encouraged them to attend university. In some cases, the mother was the only parent in the home. As previously stated, the variation in the different samples at each institution warranted a conservative method for post hoc analysis, and results should be considered in light of this major limitation.

Factorial ANOVAs (or two-way ANOVAs) using school type and mother's level of education as the indicator for first-generation-in-college student status were run in order to compare the students' responses on the scale scores by the main effects: institutional type and mother's educational level. Using this design allows for control of the influence that being a first-generation college student may have on the dependent variables. Two independent variables provide a more precise estimate of what can be gained from the comparison (McMillan & Schumacher, 2001). To identify the contrast, Scheffe's test was used because it is a more conservative post hoc analysis.

Five of the scales had no significant main effects or interaction effects. This indicates that there were no statistically significant differences among the campus environments as measured by family responsibility, academic difficulty, academic behaviors, institutional commitment, and encouragement.

The other scales indicated some significant differences and are discussed individually (Table 4.1).

There was a statistically significant difference on both personal factors measured. The statistically significant difference on ethnic identity (MEIM) obtained an F value of 5.423, *df* = 2, 503, *p* =.005. The post hoc showed that the difference was between the students in the diverse environment, with the highest mean scores (M = 42.50), and the students at the PWI, with the lowest mean scores (M = 39.64). There was also a statistically significant difference on the acculturation score (F = 15.459, *df* = 2, 502, *p* = .000) with the students at the PWI (M = 47.18) having a significantly higher mean score than the students at either the diverse (M = 35.66) or monocultural (M = 35.27) institutions.

Several of the environmental factors had statistically significant differences. Cultural affinity focuses on the presence of Latino/a faculty, staff, and students within the college environment. The mean scores on this scale also

TABLE 4.1
Main Effects of Institutional Environments

Dependent Variable	*df*	*Mean Square*	*F*	*p*	*Eta Squared* (η^2)
Acculturation (Marin et al., 1987)	2, 502	953.916	15.459	.000	.058
Ethnic Identity (Phinney, 1992)	2, 503	163.821	5.423	.005	.021
Encouragement* (Nora et al., 1997)	2, 503	25.933	1.775	.171	.007
Satisfaction With Faculty (Nora et al., 1997)	2, 503	54.451	6.694	.001	.026
Institutional Commitment (Nora et al., 1997)	2, 503	33.018	2.969	.052	.012
Academic Difficulty (Nora et al., 1997)	2, 503	4.157	.680	.507	.003
Family Responsibility (Nora et al., 1997)	2, 502	15.795	.844	.430	.003
Cultural Affinity (Nora et al., 1997)	2, 503	142.183	17.564	.000	.065
Academic Behaviors (Nora et al., 1997)	2, 502	8.395	.965	.382	.004

* This variable had an interaction effect.

had statistically significant differences (F = 17.564, *df* = 2, 503, *p* =.000), and the differences were again between the PWI students, with the lowest mean score (M = 7.11), and students from the other two environments: diverse (M = 10.52) and monocultural (M = 11.12).

A statistically significant difference was also found among the satisfaction with faculty mean scores (F = 6.694, *df* = 2, 503, *p* = .001). The post hoc analysis determined that the difference was between the PWI (M = 13.50) and the monocultural environment (M = 15.11). On the encouragement scale there was a statistically significant interaction effect that required further analysis. While there was no significant main effect by school type, the data were depicted on a line graph and frequency report to investigate the interaction. It was determined that the interaction was likely a product of the small sample size of the PWI sample and thus did not have a substantive effect on comparing the environments.

The investigation of the main effect of mother's educational level yielded no effect on the dependent variables. The only significance that emerged from the analysis was the interaction effect on the encouragement scale, which was previously discussed. The means and standard deviations for each scale by campus type can be found in Table 4.2.

Because this type of comparison is not common, there are limited comparisons to other studies that can be made. What is learned from this is that the personal characteristics differ for Latinx students among these institutional campuses. There are more acculturated students with lower ethnic identity scores in PWIs than in diverse or monocultural environments. This finding is somewhat consistent with Torres, Winston, and Cooper (2003), who compared students' ethnic identity and acculturation at urban universities and community colleges in areas with and without a critical mass of Latinos. What is most interesting about this result is that the highest level of ethnic identity was found among the students in the diverse environment. This finding would add to the understanding that increasing diversity at an institution can create a better climate for Latinx college students because they develop the critical thinking skills required to deal with differences. This could also indicate that students in diverse institutional environments may confront more dissonance and as a result may have clear choices about their sense of self as Latinx students. Because these institutions were primarily commuter institutions, the institutional environments reflected the geographic location of the colleges and likely the demographic makeup of those cities.

The differences in satisfaction could indicate that a higher structural presence of Latinx faculty and staff, as is the case for monocultural environments, has an influence on faculty satisfaction for Latinx students.

TABLE 4.2
Means and Standard Deviations by Campus Environment

Dependent Variable	*Monocultural (Mean [SD])*	*Diverse (Mean [SD])*	*Predominantly White (Mean [SD])*
Acculturation (Marin et al., 1987)	35.27 (8.46)	35.66 (8.01)	47.18 (6.79)
Ethnic Identity (Phinney, 1992)	41.31 (5.76)	42.50 (5.06)	39.64 (6.12)
Encouragement (Nora, et al., 1997)	20.93 (3.95)	21.18 (3.55)	21.21 (4.67)
Satisfaction With Faculty (Nora et al., 1997)	15.11 (3.03)	14.77 (2.55)	13.50 (2.76)
Institutional Commitment (Nora et al., 1997)	15.90 (3.45)	15.94 (3.18)	13.21 (3.62)
Academic Difficulty (Nora et al., 1997)	6.20 (2.47)	6.79 (2.59)	5.96 (2.05)
Family Responsibility (Nora et al., 1997)	9.64 (4.55)	9.82 (4.03)	9.29 (4.28)
Cultural Affinity (Nora et al., 1997)	11.12 (2.73)	10.52 (2.97)	7.11 (2.96)
Academic Behaviors (Nora et al., 1997)	11.64 (3.18)	11.49 (2.73)	10.64 (1.68)

Monocultural institutions are more likely to have Latinx faculty and staff, thus making it understandable that Latinx students in this environment would have a higher level of satisfaction with faculty. The differences registered by this scale among the institutional campuses could also be seen in conjunction with the finding that students are more likely to be satisfied overall with the institution when they have faculty that "engage in teaching and research activities that address diversity issues" (Villalpando, 2002, p. 140). In addition, there is the finding that Latinx students who perceive "a student-centered faculty and administration are more likely to be academically adjusted in the second year" of college (Hurtado et al., 1996, p. 145). The more structurally diverse an institution is, the more likely it is to have faculty that engage in activities that enforce the importance of diversity and place Latinx students at the center of their work. In this study, the monocultural institution had a high level of one type of structural diversity—a high number of Latinx faculty and staff, which likely helped students perceive a more open and potentially satisfactory environment.

In contrast, several environmental factors were not influenced by the environmental differences. These were family responsibility, academic difficulty, and institutional commitment (level of commitment a student has to completing his or her degree at that institution). The reasons for this result could be that these variables are not as influenced by outside structures, such as the number of Latinx faculty or availability of culturally specific food and entertainment. The individual focus of these dependent variables may negate the environmental differences. Another interpretation is that comparing these environments does not imply a better environment for Latinx students. The effect size indices bring into question the appropriateness of comparing these institutional campuses, and therefore only limited conclusions can be drawn.

Connections to Support Within the Environment

Considering the experiences of first-generation-in-college students is important in other ways. We wanted to consider why Latinx first-generation students craved information but often did not have behaviors that positioned them for success. In the next section, we will consider the role of having an identified mentor or adviser and using information-seeking behaviors that influence student success.

Mentoring students is an effective strategy to address the needs of college students (Torres & Hernandez, 2009). Faculty/student mentoring programs can increase students' grade point averages and lower dropout rates. The role of mentoring is important for Latinx students who need a knowledgeable guide to help them navigate institutions of higher education. Zalaquett and Lopez (2006) utilized the narrative stories of 13 Latinx students who were academically successful, were bilingual, and had demonstrated financial need to investigate the impact of college mentoring on the participants. These students' narratives described how their mentors welcomed them to the university;' acquainted them with the institution's organizational values, culture, customs, and resources; and provided advice and moral support. Mentors were also able to help integrate them into the campus community, aid in developing their confidence, and serve as a source of encouragement within the college community.

It is highly desirable for academic advising to incorporate the elements described in the mentoring process (Kuh, Kinzie, Buckley, Bridges, & Hayek, 2007). When considering advising, the quality of advising is often brought into question and determines if the adviser can serve as a mentor. Regardless of whether a Latinx student has a mentor or an assigned adviser, these individuals can play a critical support role in helping students navigate the environment.

Among the Latinx college students who responded to the survey portion of this study, it was found that in the second year of college only 42% had identified an adviser or mentor (Torres & Hernandez, 2009). Using t-test comparisons, Torres and Hernandez (2009) found that the students who had identified an adviser or mentor had statistically significantly higher scores on scales measuring satisfaction with faculty, cultural affinity, academic integration, institutional commitment, and encouragement. These scales were found to influence students' intent to persist in college (Nora et al., 1997; Torres, 2006). These results point to the importance of recreating systems that promote having an identified adviser. It is also important to understand that being assigned an adviser does not necessarily mean a student will actually use the adviser. Trust has to be built between the Latinx student and the assigned adviser.

Considering how first-generation-in-college Latinx students seek out information is also critical. Using interview data from 24 Latinx students who self-identified as being the first generation in college and who were interviewed for 3 to 4 years, 3 patterns emerged that can explain how these students sought out information about their colleges.

> 1. Students failed to recognize advisers as authority figures.
> 2. Students in this study consistently relied on information from peers, pamphlets, or staff with whom they had built a personal relationship.
> 3. Students who changed their pattern of information seeking had experienced dissonance, which for some was negative [e.g., loss of financial aid]. (Torres, Reiser, LePeau, Davis, & Ruder, 2006, p. 67)

From these patterns a model (Figure 4.1) was created to illustrate the behaviors and consequences for these students.

The model of first-generation Latinx college students' approach to seeking information illustrates the importance of making sure that institutions are explicit about the role and the need to seek out academic advising. In addition, the experiences of students seem to indicate that advisers must understand the unique cultural aspects that are critical for Latinx students. Within this study it was clear that trust and developing a relationship with an adviser/mentor was essential. While several students voiced concerns that they were getting the run around, it seemed to the group creating this model that the students did not know what questions to ask. As a result, the adviser may not have provided the information that was really needed. This may sound like an adviser has to read the minds of students, but that is not the case. Patience, time, and explicit explanations can help the adviser and the student understand what questions should be discussed.

Figure 4.1. Model of first-generation Latinx college students' approach to seeking information.

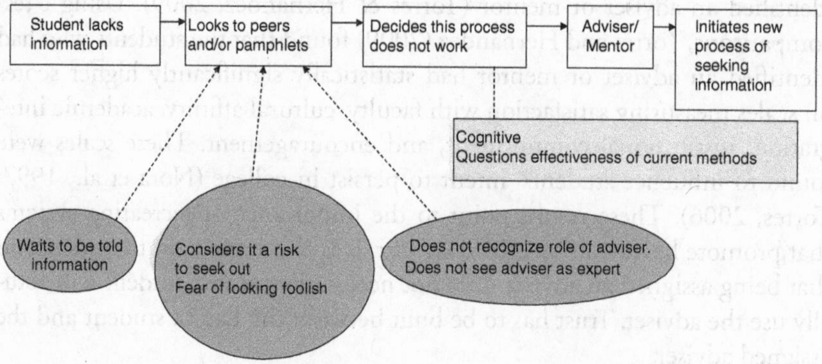

Source: Torres et al.. (2006). A model of first-generation Latino/a college students' approach to seeking academic information. *NACADA Journal, 26*(2) 65–70. Reprinted with permission from NACADA: The Global Community for Academic Advising (www.nacada.ksu.edu).

Societal Factors

It is virtually impossible to control societal factors when looking at Latinx student success, but the influence of these factors cannot be ignored. Society constructs meaning for various factors and can impose these meanings on others—regardless of whether they apply. For those from underrepresented groups, these societal constructions can serve as constant reminders of who we "are" as Latinos, but they can also be negative. The societal factor that we are labeling as socially constructed is familial expectations associated with the Latino culture.

Familial Expectations

Within the ethnic identity literature *familialism* is defined as the structure that mitigates cultural change processes, such as acculturation or ethnic identification (Keefe & Padilla, 1987; Marin, 1993). Research on Latino families found that they tend to participate in more interactions with their relatives and depend more on family members for assistance than larger institutions or groups (Marin, 1993).

Torres (2004a) found two important factors when looking at the familial expectations: the language used to self-describe students' identity and the presence of Latinos in the geographic area where the students grew up. In a previous study, Torres (2003a) identified the properties associated with the first two years of college at one PWI, but the inclusion of students from multiple contexts expanded the properties found within the dimension. In the following sections we explore the notion of acculturated parents (Torres, 2003a), environments where Latinos are a critical mass, and perceptions of how multiracial individuals perceive the environment.

The first dimension of acculturated parents (Torres, 2004a) describes students who intermingle both Latino and Anglo cultures. They are comfortable choosing from both cultures and do not feel a need to deny or neglect their culture of origin. Araceli describes the influence of her parents by saying:

> I have been raised to speak Spanish at home. I speak Spanish with 'la familia.' But yet they have always said you are Mexican, but you are American too. So don't let anyone put you down. Because you have a right just like everyone else that was born here. (Torres, 2004a, p. 463).

Her quote articulates her understanding of the intermingling of the two cultures and her sense of self in regard to her ethnicity. While Araceli is first generation in the United States, the environment that influences her perspectives has a small number of Latinos and the environment around her is predominantly White.

The second dimension is the variation of students in Latino enclaves where there are many individuals from one culture. On the surface they may appear acculturated to the American culture, yet they experience a variety of cultural conflicts when they are in the educational environment. These conflicts are not as severe as those of students from less acculturated parents, but they can influence the college experience. These students are more likely to hide their cultural conflict because they sense others may not understand or they may be ridiculed. The cultural conflicts illustrated here revolve around parental understanding and expectations. The environmental influence can be seen in the language used to self-describe. Bob is an example of how living on the border creates unique cultural conflict.

Bob simply explained, "Hispanic because I was born on this side of the United States, and Mexican because . . . everybody in my family is Mexican." While students in this geographic area comprise the majority, they seem to be burdened with the stereotype of proving their right to belong in the United States. This externally defined sense of self reflects the continuing issues that arise around immigration within this country.

The third dimension is illustrated by students who come from mixed backgrounds or are adopted by White parents. These students may not be easily identifiable because their names may not offer a clue or their appearance may not provide any indication of their background. Though these students often blend into the overall environment of their colleges, this assimilation should be considered within the context of ethnic/racial identity development (Phinney, 1993) and the possibility that identity development issues surrounding ethnicity can emerge in the future. These potential cultural conflicts could impact their college experience. It is important to provide environments for these students where they can express their uncertainties, while also being valued for however they choose to self-identify.

While taking a class from a Latinx professor, Elizabeth found herself among other Latinx students who could speak Spanish and shared some of the more common Latino phenotypes. As a self-proclaimed "half-and-half," Elizabeth had a typical Spanish surname, but her features were not typical (red hair and pale, freckled skin). She describes her interactions in her second year of college like this:

> So in that class, I just felt whiter than white, like more American than ever, and they would stay afterwards with the professor and speak Spanish and I'm just, oh I just hurt. I really want to be able to do that and that's like a really big deal why I'm studying the entire year [abroad], because my Spanish is horrendous and . . . I want to be fluent by the time I get back.

In spite of her desire to explore her Latinx identity within the college environment, specifically a course with a Latinx professor, Elizabeth felt that her inability to speak Spanish limited her ability to be a part of this group. In addition, one of the goals for her study abroad time was to be able to speak to her grandmother in Spanish—which she eventually did.

It is important to remember that as part of the development of a Latinx internalized identity, these individuals learn to manage familial expectations (Torres & Hernandez, 2007). Individuals did not see separating from or ignoring family as a viable option within their lives. Rather, the coping mechanism that developed was to manage the expectations within the individual's internalized identity.

Among the adult Latinx participants, we explored Latinas' focus on family when making meaning of their life experiences. Findings indicate that Latinas often make sense of their ethnic identity through major life events. For most of these women, the life events tended to be associated with family, such as marriage, childbearing, and negotiating relationships with family members as culture is being transmitted across several generations (Martinez, Torres, Wallace White, Medrano, Robledo, & Hernandez, 2012).

The issue of cultural conflict was mentioned in the previous section, but within the higher education literature it is an understudied construct. The next balance section uses data from the interviews to consider survey items that would measure cultural conflict.

Cultural Conflict

The concept of cultural conflict emerged in the data previously illustrated in this chapter that Latinx students perceive a balancing of the expectations between the Latino and majority (Anglo) culture.

Using a mixed-method approach the data in this study allowed for the exploration of the construct of cultural conflict among Latinx college students. During the interviews, comments and patterns of conflict between the cultures emerged, thus prompting a closer look at this construct and its potential influence on the college student experience. The exploration of this construct begins with a review of the relevant literature, and the proposed construction of items are tested using confirmatory factor analysis to measure cultural conflict among Latinx college students.

Cultural conflict originates from the idea that there is an acculturation process that occurs when two cultures are integrated. The acculturation process "always involves contact, often involves conflict, and usually results in some form of adaptation by the individual or group" (Berry, 1994, p. 125). While the outcome is always some type of adaptation to the environment, there is great variation in how this outcome can be manifested. In essence, acculturation can be seen as the adaptive process of an individual to the broader social context (Knight, Bernal, Garza, & Cota, 1993). It is the conflict inherent in the process that gives credence to cultural conflict.

While acculturation among college students can produce a particular type of stress, Torres and colleagues (2003) concluded that there was no statistically significant difference among Latinx college students' cultural orientation and their level of stress. The issues described in the literature illustrate the conflicting nature of the acculturation process and demonstrate the need to understand more about the process of negotiating two cultures. The negotiation of two cultures is also illustrated in the cultural congruence literature.

A completely different framework that focuses on college students dealing with cultural conflict comes from Gloria and Robinson Kurpius (1996), who believe that cultural congruence considers how Latinx students fit within the college environment. The fact that Latinx students experience being in two cultures (Latino and American) creates the possibility that there will be incongruence when the values, beliefs, or expectations of each culture are different. In a study of Chicano/a college students, Gloria and Robinson Kurpius (1996) created a scale to assess the "cultural ambience" (p. 537) of the university environment. The Cultural Congruence Scale (CCS) consists of 13 items that express the elements of cultural congruence within the college environment. While this scale is psychometrically strong and is created for the college population, the theoretical foundation of the scale assumes that the college environment creates potential cultural conflict rather than the cultural conflict existing regardless of context or individual.

The diversity of Latinx college students requires a broader perspective that is neither detached from nor dependent on the college environment. For many of the commuter college students, the college environment was not as critical an aspect of the higher education experiences (Torres & DeSawal, 2004). In addition, cultural conflict involves more than being in congruence with the environment; it also involves making decisions about one's culture of origin. This can represent a desire to let go of some cultural values that the individual has decided are not consistent with the identity being constructed within the context of both cultures.

The issues that emerged at the PWI included a lack of understanding for one's culture, issues of language, pressure from less acculturated parents, and making choices between the culture of origin and the predominantly White culture within the institution. Carlos illustrated the lack of understanding peers had about his culture and the differing expectations peers placed on him. Carlos explained his transition from living in an area with Latinos as the majority to the PWI like this:

> Before when I was at home everybody knew I was Hispanic. . . . Everybody knew I am Mexican and it is just part of everyday life. Now I come [to college] and I have to say my name differently. . . . I have to educate people about who I am, where I am from, what the reality of my life [is], in contrast to what they think the reality of my life is. (Torres, 2003a, p. 537)

Because the majority of students in this sample were commuter college students, the types of conflicts were different, yet they did authenticate the existence of cultural conflict.

Susie, who lived at home and attended a diverse urban university, described the conflict she felt with her parents' view of how she should live her life in the following:

> Like usually in my house my dad he encourages us to keep on going, and my mom I think she is starting to accept it. Because at first she used to [think] that woman [*sic*] were supposed to be in the kitchen cooking, and that is how we used to argue a lot, because me and my sister used to be telling my mom "Oh yeah, you want us to be in a marriage where he is beating us and all we do is cook food because it is like a cultural norm that we can't divorce or nothing like that."

Maggie also illustrated some of the conflicting issues that parents bring to the environment of a Latinx college student. She described her family's expectation by saying that "it [family] influences a lot because my dad is very strict, and well, my dad's side of the family is very strict and mom's side of the [family] is [not as much]." When asked what "strict" means, she stated that her father was "very traditional, and that girls are meant to be in the home and like that. My dad wants me to get an education though." This illustrates the dissonance that can occur as a result of being between two cultures. On the one hand, there is a desire to maintain traditional gender roles of being a stay-at-home woman. On the other hand is the recognition that in the United States an education is necessary for a career. While this dissonance can be more complex than this dichotomous illustration, it does further exemplify the existence of cultural conflicts.

This conflict also occurred for the men in the study. Miguel explained how his parents did not understand what his life was like in college. He described how he tried to communicate this to his parents:

> I just tell them, "Understand there are different pressures." Usually it is more my father, more traditional. Hard work and always working. It could be a little conflict here and there, but you know—I just try to work around it.

The validation of the construct within the qualitative samples provided the support to test nine scale items that could measure the ideas that emerged when participants described their cultural conflicts. With the larger multi-institutional survey sample, we were able to create a survey and test the validity of the items for a Latinx cultural conflict scale. The first method to verify construct validity was the confirmation of cultural conflict in both the pilot and longitudinal samples, which was done by looking at the participants' stories. The second method was to conduct a confirmatory factor analysis (CFA) to test the a priori theoretical construct. Using CFA allows the relationship between the observed variable and the underlying theoretical construct (factor) to be examined (Byrne, 1998). LISREL was used to conduct the CFA (Jöreskog & Sörbom, 2001).

The initial model using all nine items did not have a good model fit. When this occurs, it is customary to examine each item to make sure it is theoretically appropriate for the underlying construct. During this examination, five items were found to be inconsistent with the theoretical construct of cultural conflict. These items were deleted for the following reasons: (a) the wording of the item was not clearly focused on the Latino population and could apply to anyone, (b) issues regarding language were not present within the larger multi-institutional study, (c) the wording of the item was more focused on issues surrounding first-generation-in-college students than Latinx cultural conflict, and (d) one item was more focused on mitigating cultural conflict than on the conflict itself. For these reasons, five items were deleted and another CFA was conducted with the remaining four items.

These four items did illustrate an acceptable model fit. The following items were used with responses on a five-point scale ranging from strongly agree to disagree:

1. My parents' expectations for my personal life are based on their country of origin rather than U.S. culture.
2. I feel I have to balance my parents' cultural expectations with what is expected of me on campus.
3. I feel that my parents' expectations of me are different than my American friends' parents.
4. Sometimes when I am around people from my own culture, I feel comfortable and behave differently than when I'm around people who are not Latino.

Because the first two items naturally correlated, these two items could be correlated. The results of the CFA indicate a root mean square error of approximation (RMSEA) of .071, indicating an acceptable model fit (Byrne, 1998). The relative fit index (RFI) of .96 and the comparative fit index (CFI) of .99 also indicate an acceptable model fit (Hu & Bentler, 1999). These results indicate the proposed 4-item model is acceptable to explain the factor of cultural conflict among Latinx college students.

Using the four items, the internal consistency was calculated using a Cronbach alpha statistic. The scale measuring Latinx cultural conflict illustrated good internal consistency with a Cronbach alpha statistic of .739 (.74) (Leech, Barrett, & Morgan, 2005).

Because this study was longitudinal in nature, it was possible to test how consistently participants respond over time (Crocker & Algina, 1986). The test-retest method to examine internal reliability provided further evidence of the reliability of the Latinx Cultural Conflict Scale. Two factors influenced the correlation between test times. First, one year took place between testing, which could allow for maturation or changes to occur and thus lower the potential correlation. The recommended time for retesting is much shorter than one year. Second, attitude measures often have lower correlation coefficients (Crocker & Algina, 1986).

To understand how this construct influences the college experience of Latinx college students, further analyses were conducted. To consider the change in levels of cultural conflict over time, paired-sample t-tests were used to pair respondents over the four-year period. These analyses found no significant differences between the first year and any of the following years. This finding indicates that the level of cultural conflict may be constant throughout the college years. It is possible that students develop coping mechanisms to deal with cultural conflict, yet the conflict itself still exists. The key issue is that cultural conflict does not significantly diminish over time.

How environmental measures may influence the Latinx experience can also be discerned by looking at the survey data, and we used three different scales that focused on the environment to consider these differences: (a) the National Survey of Student Engagement (NSSE) Supportive Campus Environment benchmark, (b) the University Environment Scale (Gloria & Robinson Kurpius, 1996), and (c) the Latinx Cultural Conflict Scale. Tables 4.3 and 4.4 provide the results of the comparisons among the scales. The uneven cell size limits comparisons across institutional type and findings were discussed earlier in this chapter. Comparing results among years of survey administration (Table 4.4) indicated that there was no significant difference between the responses each year. Only differences between the third and fourth year of administration of the Latinx Cultural Conflict Scale approached a level of significance with .053. Overall, these results seem to indicate that the perceptions measured by these environmental scales stay fairly consistent from year to year.

One aspect to consider is that cultural conflict seems to be an internal struggle. This type of scale can be helpful in identifying the level of internal struggle a Latinx college student is having regarding the choices that must be made between the culture of origin and the culture present in the college setting. The finding that cultural conflict is more likely to be an internal struggle makes it an interesting proxy for a variety of issues. The negative correlation between cultural conflict and acculturation indicates that the lower the level of acculturation to the majority culture, the higher the level of cultural conflict.

The finding that Latinx students with first-generation immigration status in the United States have the highest mean score of cultural conflict triangulates this relationship between acculturation and cultural conflict. This is consistent with Mena, Padilla, and Maldonado's (1987) study, which also found that acculturation stress is higher in Latinx students who are first generation in the United States. The items used in this scale, along with the qualitative data, spoke to the expectations of parents for their children to maintain the cultural traditions from their country of origin. Latinx college students who have immigrant parents and have strong links to their culture of origin may feel the division between Latino and American culture most strongly, and may lack familial role models (as do second- and third-generation Latinos) to demonstrate how to successfully balance both cultures. The level of stress may be even higher for students who live with their parents, as was found in this study. The choices that they make in regard

TABLE 4.3
Means for Environmental Scales by Year and Institutional Type

Scale and Institution	*Year 2 Means (SD)*	*N*	*Year 3 Means (SD)*	*N*	*Year 4 Means (SD)*	*N*
Supportive Campus Environment (NSSE) (total number of participants)	**23.36 (5.26)**	**311**	**24.27 (5.22)**	**220**	**24.27 (4.47)**	**156**
Monocultural Institution	23.69 (5.13)	199	24.30 (5.46)	140	24.94 (4.84)	94
Diverse Institution	23.20 (5.12)	97	24.40 (4.74)	70	23.60 (4.27)	55
PWI	20.00 (6.74)	15	23.00 (5.33)	10	20.57 (4.47)	7
University Environment Scale (Gloria & Robinson Kurpius, 1996)	**59.45 (8.94)**	**311**	**60.49 (4.46)**	**220**	**60.15 (7.33)**	**156**
Monocultural Institution	59.77 (9.20)	199	60.49 (7.46)	140	59.85 (8.06)	94
Diverse Institution	58.97 (8.62)	97	60.20 (7.11)	70	60.55 (6.19)	55
PWI	58.27 (7.71)	15	59.00 (5.91)	10	61.14 (5.60)	7
Latinx Cultural Conflict Scale	**11.10 (3.69)**	**311**	**11.21 (3.73)**	**220**	**10.86 (2.54)**	**156**
Monocultural Institution	10.76 (3.86)	199	10.94 (3.90)	140	10.57 (3.55)	94
Diverse Institution	11.66 (3.19)	97	11.87 (3.40)	70	11.64 (3.19)	55
PWI	11.93 (4.20)	15	10.50 (3.31)	10	10.96 (2.54)	7

Note: The three scales used to consider environmental influences are the Supportive Campus Environment from the National Survey of Student Engagement, the University Environment Scale, and the new Latinx Cultural Conflict Scale.

to their acculturation to U.S. culture and maintenance of Latino culture in order to be successful in college also has implications for their family life.

While the level of cultural conflict has been shown to not diminish over time, administrators and faculty can assist Latinx students in

TABLE 4.4
Campus Environment Scales Paired T-Test By Year

Paired T-Test (n)	*Year 1 Mean (SD) to Year 2*	*Statistic of Interest (df)*	*Significance*
Supportive Campus Environment *(NSSE)*			
Year 2 to Year 3 (227)	23.81 (4.99) to 24.26 (5.16)	-1.379 (226)	.169
Year 3 to Year 4 (155)	24.04 (5.35) to 24.06 (4.88)	-.075 (154)	.940
University Environment Scale (Gloria & Robinson Kurpius, 1996)			
Year 2 to Year 3 (209)	59.63 (8.78) to 60.38 (7.21)	-1.29 (208)	.198
Year 3 to Year 4 (149)	60.51 (7.42) to 60.31 (7.10)	.338 (148)	.736
Latinx Cultural Conflict Scale			
Year 2 to Year 3 (231)	11.20 (3.81) to 11.24 (3.67)	-.148 (230)	.883
Year 3 to Year 4 (168)	11.54 (3.64) to 11.01 (3.41)	1.946 (167)	.053

managing this conflict by recognizing the additional stress that first-generation immigrant Latinos may experience as they negotiate acculturating to mainstream culture while maintaining their parents' cultural expectations. Student services professionals should be sensitive to cultural choices made to adapt to college expectations and norms that may cause cultural conflict for Latinx students and their relationships with their parents. This is especially poignant for first-generation immigrant Latinx. Understanding some of the implications around cultural choices, such as living away from home or deviating from traditional gender roles, can help faculty and administrators facilitate a more culturally relevant conversation with these students.

Summary of Environmental Influences on Latinx Experiences

This chapter highlights several interesting environmental factors that influence the student experience. Following are the lessons to apply from this chapter.

1. The idea that person-environment fit is highly desirable as a positive predictor of student success was challenged. While this level of "fit" has its positive points, this study indicates that a perfect fit may not be as desirable as once thought since students are not challenged to consider different contexts than what they previously knew.
2. Findings from this study indicate that ensuring Latinx college students have an assigned adviser or mentor is critical to their success in college. The difference on measures that can influence student success illustrates that students who seek assistance from a mentor or adviser are more likely to be successful.
3. Advisers cannot assume first-generation-in-college Latinx students will understand their role and seek them out for advice. The "we have built it, they will come" approach to advising does not work for these students, and it is critical to understand how to develop a trusting relationship.
4. Familial expectations are not ignored, but creating ways to manage those expectations does allow individuals to further develop their own internalized sense of self.
5. While cultural conflict may be an internal struggle, it is important for practitioners and faculty to understand how these conflicts can influence how Latinx college students view their experiences.

5

INTERSECTIONS OF MULTIPLE IDENTITIES AND CONTEXTUAL INFLUENCES

Due to increasing efforts to create and revise developmental theories to be more inclusive of minoritized populations and take into consideration the ways that privilege and oppression affect development, scholars have been tasked to "dig deeper into the messiness and complexity that is the developmental process of individuals who hold multiple identities, straddle privileged and marginalized statuses simultaneously, and live their lives moving from one context to the other" (Hernández, 2017, p. 216). Scholars who have done this messy work of examining identity development revealed significant insights the ways how social location plays a substantial role in how individuals make meaning of their multiple identities, as well as how they manage these identities in relationships with classmates, friends, family members, and others (Jones, 2009). The concept of social location comes from sociological perspectives which consider social structures and other elements that situate identity groups within the complex dynamics of race and ethnicity in the United States. In the sample of college students in these studies, we found that in some spaces Latino identity was a marginalized identity susceptible to negative stereotyping; in other spaces being Latino granted students connection, understanding, and other privileges. Understanding that their identities are grounded in social locations in conjunction with the contexts in which these students interact provides a much richer understanding of their journey as Latinx students.

Few scholars within the higher education field are engaging with the complexity of social location. Those who are have expanded the idea that identity is closely related to the context in which we enact our sense of self. These studies concluded that context interacts with dimensions of identity and influences the meaning-making individuals are constantly negotiating and managing when more than one identity may be salient at a time (Jones, 2009; Jones & Abes, 2013; Jones, Kim, & Skendall, 2012).

In this chapter we review how we dove into the messiness of examining development via multiple contexts and identities (e.g., gender, sexual orientation, class, ethnicity, and race, to name a few). The examination into the ways that multiple identities intersect, clash, and influence each other was critical to unpack the complexity of Latino identity development and answered the call to create developmental theories that validate the developmental processes of often invisible populations (Hernandez, 2017), such as minoritized sexual identities, Latinx, or nontraditional Latinx college students. In this chapter, we share our analysis of multiple identities as further evidence to confirm the powerful role that context (within their communities, college environments, and family) and the social forces of privilege and marginalization play in how Latinos made meaning of their identities. First, we begin with the results of the analyses conducted to examine specific populations in our study. Then, we explain the results as they relate to confirming and challenging the lifespan Latinx identity development model. Finally, we offer two students' stories to illustrate how Latino identity development connected to making meaning of their other identities.

Initial Investigation of Latinos' Multiple Identities

In the analyses that ultimately resulted in the lifespan model of Latinx identity development, we intentionally investigated the possibility of different developmental processes for particular populations. To be clear, this analysis of multiple identities did not make our work intersectional. We did not employ intersectionality as a theoretical perspective; rather, we were focused on influences by institutional type and other contextual factors. Doing intersectionality research requires implementation of its core tenets to the research approach, design, and implementation. One of these tenets is to move away from focusing on a singular identity and instead examine multiple identities in order to uncover how power and privilege function and are perpetuated in society (Dill & Zambrana, 2009). Our approach was decidedly nonintersectional as we consistently placed Latino ethnic identity as central to our work. This decision aligned with our key assumption that Latino identity is a dominant identity that is central to lived experiences and meaning-making. Its saliency in identity development is a result of our marginalized status in American society—we are consistently marked as "other" due to our appearance, accents, names, immigration histories, and negative stereotypes.

The longitudinal study's diverse sample allowed us to investigate multiple identities because it included the voices of Latinos from different regions of the United States who attend a diverse mix of institutions. The sample represented first-, second-, and third-generation immigrants and a range of accents, social classes, and ages. Some came from diverse urban settings, and others came from predominantly White suburbs. Considering that Latino ethnic identity includes individuals who represent a broad range of skin tones and national origins, in addition to the identities mentioned previously, the Latino population is quite a diverse group. For this reason, we have cautioned educators that not all Latinos have the same issues and needs when it comes to supporting their success in college (Torres, 2004b). This made us question if a single model could be useful to depict the development of a group that is so diverse and includes so many different connecting identities.

To begin the investigation, we sought to see if, and how, college context might play a role in development. Drawing from scholarship that has found that students from different racial/ethnic groups report substantially different perceptions about campus climate, incidents of racism, and sense of belonging by institution type (Nelson Laird, Bridges, Morelon-Quainoo, Williams, & Salinas Holmes, 2007), and that Latinos' sense of identity can be strongly informed by where they grew up and campus environment (Torres, 2003a), we divided the participants in the qualitative longitudinal study by institution type. Next, we examined the developmental charts that depicted students' cognitive, identity, and interpersonal development for each year they participated in the study. Considering our conclusion that context plays a central role in identity development, it was prudent to examine if certain institution types (predominantly White, diverse, or monocultural Latino) might promote growth or stymie development. In our analysis, we sought out any differences in participants' development, which we measured as developmental growth (magnitude of development of an internalized informed Latino identity as measured by phases depicted in their developmental charts), developmental status (final developmental status), or developmental markers (factors that contributed to their development and/or indicators that illustrated how they experienced that phase). Surprisingly, no differences were seen among the contexts regarding these three measures of developmental growth. No context appeared to promote or hinder development toward an internalized sense of self.

Considering the developmental scholarship that describes different developmental processes by gender, we then conducted a similar analysis to determine if there were differences in developmental growth between men and women in the study. We were curious to discover if the men and women in the longitudinal study exhibited different meaning-making processes due to socialized gendered norms and expectations as found in other studies (Baxter Magolda, 1992; Belenky, Clinchy, Goldberger, & Tarule, 1986; Harris, 2010) or if there were differences in developmental gains and/or endpoints. Again, no discernable differences were found between the groups.

We reflected on what could explain these results. One potential explanation could be that neither institution type nor gender plays a significant role in development. This conclusion would challenge prior research that determined institutional type characteristics, such as campus culture, matter for Latinx students' ethnic identity development, as well as scholarship that insists that gender must be considered in identity development. These were not conclusions that we were comfortable making, however.

This puzzle of explaining why our analysis of subgroups yielded no significant results challenged us to revisit and critically unpack our assumptions about Latina/o identity development that guided our work, specifically how we conceptualize identity development and what might promote its development. Drawing from three key assumptions derived from the review found in chapter 2 of Latina/o identity development scholarship that informed our study, we applied these assumptions to each set of analyses as a framework for plausible explanation.

Four factors contribute to the ethnic identity development of Latinos: they are (a) environment where individuals grow up, (b) generational status in the U.S., (c) self-perception of social status, and (d) college environment. These four factors contribute to identity development because they all contribute to the level of saliency that ethnic identity has on Latinx students. Saliency of identity emerges when one feels othered, or unlike those around them. Experiencing a high level of saliency of one particular social identity promotes one to make meaning of that identity, which can make other identities less conspicuous, or even invisible (Abes & Jones, 2004). Individuals then engage in a meaning-making process where they question what their Latino identity means to them, test out negative stereotypes, and examine the oppression or privilege they experience as a result.

Applying this key assumption of identity development to explain our analysis on developmental differences by institution type helps explain why we did not find any discernable differences in development for Latinos by institution type. The level of identity saliency is not bound to particular environments, but the extent to which one might feel "othered" in that particular environment. We realize that all but one of the institutions would be characterized as commuter, with students coming from the immediate area. For some students, going to a PWI may not create critical dissonance if they feel that they are going from one familiar environment to another. They might have been used to going to school with mostly White students and have had few students of color to connect with, therefore the saliency of their Latino identity may not emerge. However, some students going to the very same PWI might experience critical dissonance. If they had gone from attending a racially/ethnically diverse school to a PWI, they might feel simultaneously hypervisible and culturally isolated. In this scenario, the college environment would play a significant role in their development because it is constantly causing the dissonance that promotes their development. Therefore, analyzing participants by institutional type may not yield developmental differences because development is not promoted by institution type, but rather by the extent to which such an environment may cause a student to feel othered and make their Latino identity a highly salient part of who they are.

Development occurs when individuals engage in the meaning-making process of their lived experiences, not merely from living through the experiences. This second assumption goes hand in hand with the first, demonstrating the developmental linkage between experience and meaning-making, both of which must occur to promote the developmental process. In reviewing the insignificant findings from the exploration of gender differences in our sample, one potential explanation is that even though the participants experienced gendered family roles, sexism, and cultural expectations based on their gender, they may not have engaged in substantial meaning-making of their gender identity. Like other studies in which women did not identify or easily articulate how their gender impacted their lives (Delgado Bernal, 1997; Johnson-Bailey, 1999), the Latinx participants may not have the opportunity to make meaning of their gender identity and then subsequently articulate them in their interviews.

Change in the context influenced the level of dissonance felt and the meaning-making process for the few students who transferred institutions. Both the undergraduate longitudinal study and the adult Latinx study illustrated that change in context prompted dissonance in what was believed to be the norm. As stated previously, without this change in context the meaning-making process was not initiated. Three of the four urban universities in the undergraduate longitudinal study were considered commuter institutions where students continued to live in similar contexts with access to similar support systems. For the few students who transferred during their college career, this dissonance did prompt the meaning-making process and the process of incorporating new ideas about self. Depending on the contextual change, various responses were generated, but it was difficult to tie these changes to the institutional type. It seemed to be more about the change in environment.

Latinos' Narratives of Multiple Identities

While the institutional type and gender aspects did not yield discernable developmental differences, the sample included narratives of students who engaged with more than one social identity. In this section we continue the examination of Latinas'/os' multiple identities with the narratives of Tristan and Kathy. These narratives illustrate the centrality of Latino identity in identity development, highlighting the ways that their ethnic identity was consistently salient in their meaning-making and served as a filter through which they viewed their multiple social identities. These voices reveal the circumstances that promoted critical dissonance from family dynamics, interaction with the Latino community, and change in environments (e.g., one's neighborhood or work environment). These narratives demonstrate the multiple identities that Latinos hold, and how these identities further complicate their sense-making of what their Latino identity means to them.

Tristan

Tristan identified as Mexican and as a second-generation immigrant. A first-generation college student, he started out as a graphic design major but switched to undeclared when he was out of sequence in his major program. At the beginning of his college experience, he shared that his sexual identity was a significant issue for him, as he recognized how his traditional parents would take the news. In reflecting on his feelings that propelled him to come out as gay to his parents in his second year in college, he considered how being gay would make it impossible to live out his parents' expectations for continuing a traditional Mexican family structure:

> I had this feeling. . . . The only way I can describe it is like suffocation. Because I would go home and [my parents] would talk to me and I would realize they weren't really talking to me, they were talking to who they thought I was. . . . One morning I woke up and it wasn't like a panic attack—it was more like I broke down emotionally. I can't deal with this anymore because it felt like I was having this big, big burden. Especially for my mom. She kept asking me if I was dating any girls, or who I wanted to marry. She wanted me to marry a Mexican girl. So it kind of broke my heart to have to tell them this.

Tristan's parents did not take him coming out very well. His parents' homophobic fears about Tristan's potential influence on his younger siblings resulted in discussions about moving the family back to Mexico so his younger siblings could have a "more conservative upbringing." In addition, his parents sought out the counsel of their priest, but they were surprised when the priest turned out not to be as conservative as they hoped.

To help cope with his parents' negative reactions to his sexual identity, Tristan found support from other family members to whom he had come out earlier. As time went on, he realized that despite his parents' strong reaction to him coming out, they did truly love him and wanted the best for him. In his third year, he reported that the family expectations his parents had for him and his siblings were not exactly what he wanted for himself, but they came from a place of care and a desire for him and his siblings to have a good life. This realization put him on the path toward rebuilding his relationship with his parents, which he reflected in the following:

> [I was rebelling] just against the structure they were trying to set up for the children. I think I was kind of resentful at first because I thought that I didn't ask for this. And I just wanted to do something different. And now I see what they've set up for us and I actually do really appreciate it. And it's like, whoa, I see what [my parents] are talking about and I want to help. Now that I'm in the right state of mind to appreciate it, I'm going to dive in and help [with the family restaurant].

In reviewing Tristan's interviews from year to year, it is evident that his family was at the center of his life, and his parents played a significant part in his Latino identity development. His parents clearly placed cultural expectations on him, defining for him what they believed a Latino man and son should be. When he came out as gay, he expressed his sadness over crushing his mother's hopes that he would marry a nice Mexican girl and essentially carry on the family's culture and values. For him, his Latino identity developmental processes included redefining what Latino meant to him by redefining his role as a son and redefining his relationship with his parents built on more authentic understanding of each other. His gay identity was certainly a salient identity throughout this process, but his Latino identity stayed a central part of his development.

Kathy

Throughout her college experience, Kathy struggled with others' perceptions about her ethnic identity. While she self-identified as Dominican and felt strongly connected to her Latino culture, many people assumed she identified as African American. Kathy knew she did not have the stereotypical features of a Latina, but it still troubled her that her ethnic identity was often mistaken. In her first year of college, she shared this experience: "Most people that come up to me actually think that I'm African American. . . . As soon as they hear me speak Spanish they may ask me, 'Where are you from again?'"

Because being identified as Dominican was important to her, she would often assert her ethnic identity by speaking Spanish or correcting other people's assumptions.

When Kathy moved her second year to attend a different university, she found herself in a community where it seemed people were even more likely to assume that she was African American, thereby making her feel her Latina identity was even less visible. She grew to recognize the racism and negative stereotyping embedded in people's comments about her looks; people seemed unable to comprehend the possibility that Latinas could be dark-skinned too, or they gave the backhanded compliment of calling her a pretty Black woman. In her fourth year of college, she shared:

> People go to my store [in predominantly African American neighborhood] and they're just like, "Oh my God. Your hair is so long and you're so pretty to be Black." And I'm like, oh God. What is that supposed to mean? I don't even want to say I'm not Black because then it makes it seem like everyone who is Black can't be pretty and have long hair. . . . I'm not comfortable with it; to try and suggest something else would only make the situation worse. Because when they say "The Black girl with the pretty long hair" and then I'm like "Well, I'm not Black. What are you trying to say? Black people can't have long hair?". . . I'm not correcting them because it only makes the situation worse.

For Kathy, her Latina identity was consistently salient because it was a part of her that consistently was not validated. Moving to a different city and living in a predominantly Black neighborhood made it even more salient because fewer people identified her as Dominican, invalidating her identity even more. In addition, she dealt with people's racist ideas about Black people, such as Black people not being as pretty or having long hair. She could not define herself via external messages because the messages she was receiving were racist.

Kathy's narrative is important to understand because it illustrates the diversity within the Latino community. Her narrative brings a more inclusive understanding of Latino identity in two ways. One, it broadens our understanding of what Latino can be. Often, studies on Latino identity development fail to include voices of those who discuss how their features (e.g., hair, phenotype) might serve as markers for inclusion to or exclusion from the Latino community, both by fellow Latinos and non-Latinos. A failure to include these factors does not allow opportunity to acknowledge, much less carefully consider, the ways that colorism within the Latino community might affect identity development (Golash-Boza & William Darity, 2008). Two, Kathy's narrative strongly supports differentiation of race and ethnicity (Johnston-Guerrero, 2016). Latino identity is often racialized, meaning it is considered as a racial category, not an ethnicity. This practice does not allow for examining the racial differences in the Latino community, such as Latinos who identity as White, Black, Asian, Mestizo, and so on.

Latino Identity as Central in the Meaning-Making Process

Tristan's and Kathy's narratives demonstrate the diversity within the Latino community by the multiple social identities they possess in addition to their shared ethnic identity. They were chosen for the examination of how multiple social identities might affect Latinos' identity development because they discussed through the years of the study how they made meaning of their identities and how their meaning-making evolved. These narratives also illustrated how Latino identity development remained central in their meaning-making while they dealt with heterosexism and racism. For example, as Tristan struggled with coming out to his parents and dealing with their homophobic fears, his Latino identity remained central to his meaning-making process. His struggles with his parents coming to terms with his sexual identity were steeped in cultural expectations, demonstrating how his Latino identity remained central to his meaning-making process. His struggles were not just about coming out but coming out in a Latino family with parents who expected him to marry a nice Mexican girl and carry on the family's cultural traditions and values.

Kathy's narrative also demonstrated the centrality of Latino identity in her development. Unlike Tristan, who was constantly dealing with his parents' cultural expectations for him, Kathy did not have constant external expectations of others to maintain Latino cultural norms because few identified her as Latina. The change in context increased the difference in external expectations, even though she placed her Latina identity as central to her meaning-making. In her narrative, she constantly questioned how much she needed validation from others to recognize her as a Dominican woman and if verbally claiming her Latina identity would indirectly reinforce racist beliefs about African Americans.

Within the studies that influenced the development of the lifespan model are other examples of role management, language, or immigration status influencing the meaning-making process of the Latinx participants.

Several students talked about their nontraditional Latino features (looking more White than Latino) influencing how others saw them, but these individuals did not deal with having racist external beliefs applied to them. These tensions in participants' lives can be seen in the short narratives written about the students in the longitudinal study in chapter 2.

This chapter sought to complicate Latino identity development by examining how multiple identities provide the experiences that can propel or stymie development. Our analyses sought to find differences in development by comparing students who attend different institutional types and by comparing developmental differences by gender, but the analyses yielded no significant differences. This finding challenged us to further investigate how Latinos' multiple social identities might influence their development. As we reviewed the narratives of two participants in our longitudinal study, we recognized how saliency of identity promoted development. This high level of identity saliency can be caused by challenging family dynamics or interactions with strangers who fail to see who one really is. This can result in dissonance, which then promotes identity development. These narratives proved that dissonance can occur in any kind of space, or in interactions with loved ones or strangers. Looking back, it makes sense that our initial analyses, in which we sought to compare different context and gender, did not yield the type of differences expressed in other research. It is not the differences that promote development—rather it is *feeling different* that does.

The Latino community is very diverse—it represents many nationalities, immigration histories, races, sexual identities, and so on. This chapter recognizes the multiple identities represented in a population that is often presented as homogenous. By failing to acknowledge the diversity among us in sampling and failing to discuss our multiple identities in a significant way, researchers can perpetuate the norming of Latinos as Mexican, light brown-skinned, and heterosexual. In this chapter, we complicated the representation of Latinos to not only be more inclusive but also acknowledge the reality of how diverse we are, even if it results in making our work more difficult, complicated, and "messy."

6

INFLUENCES ON THE PERSISTENCE OF LATINX STUDENTS IN HIGHER EDUCATION

Although Latinx students represent the second largest student group within higher education, they tend to be concentrated in certain types of institutions. Approximately 60% of Latinx undergraduates are enrolled in HSIs, which are predominantly public, located in urban areas, and commuter institutions. The number of HSIs are almost evenly split between community colleges and four-year institutions (Santiago et al., 2016). This profile for Latinx students requires that persistence be considered differently than what is explained in traditional retention theories. In fact, more current research has found that Tinto's (1993) theory "lacks explanatory power in commuter institutions" because studies of these institutions do not support the propositions in this often-cited retention theory (Braxton, Doyle, Hartley III, Hirschy, Jones, & McLendon, 2014, pp. 79).

Models have been tested on commuter students (Bean & Metzner, 1985), and the proposition of academic and social integration may be applied to ethnically diverse campuses (Murguia, Padilla, & Pavel, 1991; Nora, 1987). These studies have also been critiqued for assuming that integration is the expectation—that students will adapt to the culture of the campus (Tanaka, 2002) or enter college and adapt to the dominant cultural frame (Tierney, 1992).

Using mixed-methods in our study allowed for a much more nuanced view of persistence or intent to persist among Latinx students at these commuter institutions. By beginning the process with listening to the stories told through the data gathered during interviews and then conceptualizing the results into a retention model, the model could reflect a culturally sensitive reality. For example, students in the qualitative phase seldom mentioned prior academic performance as critical to their success. These students reflect the posttraditional student profile that includes elements such as first in their family to enroll in college; worked for pay 30 hours or more; and chose college based on cost, proximity to family, and accessibility (Santiago et al., 2016). This profile illustrates that institutional fit was not as critical as other factors (Braxton et.al., 2014), because the choice to be at an urban university was based on family expectations to live at home and the relatively low cost of attending an urban university (as opposed to other universities in the area or within the state). As an example, one student thought about pursuing a particular major, but when he found out it was not offered at his urban university he settled on another major. Students were not as concerned with whether they "fit" into the environment as much as whether they understood how to navigate the system. While these issues can be intertwined, researchers seem to interpret "fit" as choosing from many options. Yet for these students, cultural or family reasons dictated a limited range of college choice options (Torres, 2006).

The mixed-methods data presented here will provide the qualitative evidence from the students' stories and the model creation that emerged from those stories. This work comes from a 2006 article; therefore, methodological information on the mixed-methods design is not presented and readers should reference Torres (2006). The unique nature of a retention model focused solely on Latinx student stories and using a mixed-methods design to create the model merits closer attention.

Latinx Student Stories

The qualitative analysis of the interviews illustrated that these students had a different perception of the college environment than much of what the literature and studies on traditional age students describe. This section summarizes the three themes that emerged as prevalent influences on students' college experience around persistence. The first theme, describing the hectic nature of students' lives at urban commuter universities, was "come to class and leave." The second was the lack of confidence felt when students saw themselves as "unsure I could make it." And the final theme illustrates that students wanted institutional agents to "show me the way" in order to create cognitive maps to help them maneuver the college environment.

Come to Class and Leave

Like many posttraditional students at commuter institutions, the stories illustrate multiple priorities, and being in college serves as one of many commitments Latinx students maintain. In his first year, Oscar was asked what he thought was helpful and what things he wished were different about the college environment at his university. He responded by saying: "I usual [*sic*] just come for classes, and just leave. So I don't think I can really answer that." While he noticed the opportunities available to him, he also noted that he did not have the time to participate. Oscar worked off-campus and felt he had to maintain his number of work hours in order to meet his financial obligations. Jennifer also struggled to think about what was helpful during her college experience and stated, "I really don't understand when they say college experience because I just go to school. I go to class, and then I am out of here."

Other Latinx students responded to this question with simple descriptions like, "It is nice" or "calm" on campus. It was clear that although these students wanted to better themselves through education, the traditional views of college life were not really applicable and, in some cases, not desired. Additional probes during the interviews allowed more specific issues to emerge that provided insight into the students' perception of college life. These culturally sensitive explorations confirmed that the messages were focused on failing academically and thus prepared students to have low expectations of themselves and the academic environment.

Unsure I Could Make It

Several of the students had not experienced academic success in high school but were doing much better in college. This was not the case for all of the students interviewed, but this theme highlighted that institutional stereotyping does happen in society, and as a result low expectations are set for underrepresented students (Steele & Aronson, 1995). Susie was a student who had a difficult time in high school but changed her attitude and behavior in college. As she put it:

> High school was more for me a social scene than going to learn. . . . In high school you . . . are willing to cut, we usually didn't get attention. The only attention we got was from security. . . . They . . . take our IDs away. . . . All they do . . . is single us out from the rest of the class. (Torres, 2006, p. 305)

The combination of low expectations and lack of encouragement Susie experienced did nothing to promote behavior that would lead to academic success. In the interview she was asked what made a difference for her. Susie responded by saying that she was tired of that lifestyle and that "being in college, I finally realized education is important." She recognized that, as a result of the low expectations in her high school, she was not academically prepared for college level courses but made a decision to seek out help.

Susie found support through an academic assistance program designed specifically for Latinx students at her urban university. Susie said that her program adviser helped her find tutoring and connected her to people "that are going to be beneficial to my career." The mentoring relationship helped her to see the future in a different light.

Another student, Colleen, shared that in high school most of her teachers assumed she was cutting class even when she had a legitimate reason for her absence. Colleen assumed she would not be seen as a legitimate student because at the end of high school she had a 2.1 GPA and knew she did not have the financial means to attend college. For these reasons, she did not seriously think about enrolling in college. The difference in her attitude occurred when one of her teachers reached out to her and let her know that her financial difficulties should not stand in her way of going to college. She described the interaction by saying:

> In my junior year [of high school], my earth science teacher, he was the one that kind of pushed me to go to college. He saw that I was doing good in earth science and he wanted me to become an earth science major. And he went here and started talking to me about here [university] and at the same time he was telling me about some type of tuition merit waiver. (Torres, 2006, p. 305)

Colleen applied to the honors program and maintained a 3.5 GPA in her first year of college. She continued to stay in touch with her mentor and continued to rely on him for information and advice about maneuvering the system within the university.

When students who had not done well in high school were asked what made a difference, they repeatedly referenced a mentor or faculty member who believed in them and encouraged them to attend college. As a result of this relationship with a mentor, they were prompted to change their expectations about education and were also able to adjust their behavior in order to focus on being a good student. Even students with good grades referenced adults who helped them figure out the system. While the good students did not experience the same academic difficulties as Susie or Colleen, they talked about not knowing how to do things in college and uncertainty about whether they would do well in the new environment. These comments illustrate the insecure feelings many first-generation college students experience, yet the feelings are further exasperated when there is less cultural congruency in the environment.

Show Me the Way

These students repeatedly referenced mentors, special academic assistance programs, and faculty as making a difference in their college experience. These programs provided several helpful elements including having students around like themselves, one-on-one attention, and the ability to get specialized academic help. Danneal, although not required to enter a special program (GPA entrance criteria), chose to enroll in the same program as Susie because she "felt like maybe being in a little bit more around my people [Latinos], and more like one-on-one counseling, it would help me a great deal" (Torres, 2006, p. 306). She went on to describe that the personal attention made a difference for her and allowed her to feel more comfortable with being a college student. Rachel also entered an academic support program by being part of a cohort in one of the schools within the university. She found that the friendships she made within her cohort helped her through her academic difficulties and made her feel part of a community.

Students also referenced individual faculty as being helpful and willing to assist them outside the classroom. Faculty availability on these urban campuses emerged as a major positive influence for these students. Isis talked about the interactions with the faculty by saying: "The teachers are more . . . into the students" (Torres, 2006, p. 306). Roberto described college as "more challenging than high school. . . . So far, all my teachers have been a lot of help" (Torres, 2006, p. 306). In Roberto's case a peer mentor program was helpful and allowed him to talk to older peers who provided advising about academics and other concerns. Not all of the universities provided this level of help, however. Panfilo mentioned that he had to search for tutorial help, but once he found the supplemental instruction (SI) sections he felt like they provided the assistance he needed. The SI focused on a learning community model and provided support in gatekeeper courses where students had difficulty being successful.

Connections with faculty and mentors were made through either students' academic adviser or on-campus job. Isis had a work-study job in an academic department and because she often worked alone she reflected on the issues connected to her studies. In addition, she found that the faculty in the department were helpful. "They give me advice. . . . It helps, because you keep on thinking about what it is that is going on" (Torres, 2006, p. 306). Nonacademic jobs on campus also help. Manuela worked a few hours a week at the university bookstore and found that knowing what courses are offered and the books being used "helps me understand a lot" (Torres, 2006, p. 306).

Strong ethnic support systems assisted students when they were away from the college setting. Continuing to live at home, rather than leaving to go away to college allowed for these support systems to be maintained. Students describe their social support as being outside the college environment. The family was their central social support system, and social relationships within their communities were more supportive than those within the college environment. Most of the students felt their families were supportive but did not necessarily understand their experiences in college. The tension between support and understanding created cultural issues for students. For example, Maria explained the cultural conflict with expectations of college life. For Maria, this type of conflict emerged when she had to attend an out-of-class group meeting:

> They are so strict. I have to sometimes go to meetings and projects and they are like—'well no' and I am like, well this is different. It is not high school, it is not grammar school. It is college, I need to go out. (Torres, 2006, p. 307)

The idea of this conflictual feeling is consistent with the idea of internal cultural conflict discussed in chapter 5.

Integrating the Stories With Quantitative Data

Based on the themes that emerged, the traditional predictors of retention such as previous academic performance or measures of academic achievement (Nora et al., 1997; Tinto, 1993) did not seem to be the most important factors influencing student success in this context. Instead, campus experiences emerged as being more important to helping these students stay in college. Analysis of the student stories focused on how students saw themselves within the college environment and the level of support they were able to gain from positive contacts they made with adult figures that could help them figure out the system. The majority of the students in the qualitative portion of this study seldom mentioned their deficiencies and tended to see their previous academic performance in light of the stereotype imposed on them of low achievers and resulting low expectations from high school teachers; these interpretations are consistent with other research on minority students (Immerwahr, 2003; Tierney, 2000). Other research has found that the campus environments were a stronger influence on institutional commitment than student entry characteristics (Strauss & Volkwein, 2004). In their propositions about student departure at commuter institutions, Braxton and colleagues (2014) assert imperatives to support efforts to increase retention. These imperatives focus on institutions helping students feel respected and valued as learners within the institution.

The deficiency lens that focuses on what characteristics Latinx students do not possess (income, social capital, etc.) is not congruent with a culturally relevant view of the student stories and does not explain why some students succeed despite these limitations. What is critical for minority students is "how they negotiate these conflicts and how much support students receive from significant others for college attendance" (Braxton et al., 2004, p. 50). These caveats in the literature warrant the use of a different lens.

A Different Theoretical Lens

The student stories reflected the concept of self-efficacy. While many researchers consider self-efficacy, few recognize that this is only one portion of a larger theoretical lens proposed by Bandura (1986). The theoretical lens that includes self-efficacy is social cognitive theory which advocates that people function (make choices) as a result of the interaction among behavior, cognitive and personal factors, and environmental influences (Bandura, 1986). Social cognitive theory explains human functioning (choices) in terms of the "triadic reciprocality in which behavior, cognitive and other personal factors, and environmental events all operate as interacting determinants of each other" (Bandura, 1986, p. 18).

Social cognitive theory views the nature of people as defined by their capacity to (a) symbolize, (b) have forethought, (c) learn vicariously, (d) self-regulate behavior, and (e) self-reflect on their experiences (Bandura, 1986). The development of these capacities can permit people to achieve their goals. While many of these students did not have these capabilities when they began college, it was the ability to develop these capacities that allowed them to stay in college. The majority of the students, approximately 77%, were first-generation-in-college students. This factor alone may limit their ability to create positive symbols about how to maneuver the college maze and how to stay motivated in order to persist through the college years. In addition, the low expectations in high school may not promote the level of cognitive development needed to create symbols and have forethought that would transcend their present experiences and allow them to envision a different reality or life goal. The inability to create positive symbols about alternative life paths impacts their ability to have forethought about what to expect in the college environment (Bandura, 1986). Forethought can also influence the college choice process because more selective colleges require students to apply early and will not consider students after certain deadlines. For some of these students, the possibility of college attendance is not considered until after their high school graduation, and their choice is also dependent on their family responsibilities.

Within education there is much emphasis placed on experiential learning, yet few of the Latinx students in this study were provided the opportunity to learn about college experientially. Instead, they were dependent on vicarious learning, which occurs through observing others' behavior and assessing the consequences. Many of the students spoke about their parents' desire for them to have a better life. By observing the difficulties their parents experienced without an education, they recognize the need for education, but there are few role models for them to observe that would illustrate an alternative life path that includes education. Often, these students enter the college environment with few tangible expectations and do not know what to ask for if they need assistance. The lack of mentors, role models, or advisers can influence their self-regulatory and self-reflective capabilities. These capacities impact students' self-efficacy to be successful in college. In order to maintain congruence, they conform their behavior to those erroneous thoughts that they are not meant to be students (Bandura, 1986). The ability to help students create positive images and capacities is critical to their ability to reconstruct their self-image and change their behavior to ensure success (Torres & Baxter Magolda, 2004). The students who were able to develop these capabilities in the college environment were better able to describe the behaviors needed to succeed.

While determinants such as entry skills, emotional ties, and personal standards are difficult to gauge and control, institutions can manipulate social or environmental determinants to positively impact students. Contact with mentors, advisers, and faculty should be seen as a mechanism for fortuitous encounters that can positively impact students' social cognitive capabilities (Bandura, 1986).

The student stories illustrate the relationship among the concepts of social cognitive theory. The themes that emerged from the interviews had several commonalities with the concepts in Bandura's (1986) theory. The decision was made to use social cognitive theory as a framework to determine how to configure a model that considers influences on the intent to persist for these students. Using the qualitative data as a guide, the elements of the model were reconfigured. The following section connects the emergent themes to aspects of social cognitive theory.

Environmental Influences

The themes of "come to class and leave" and "unsure I could make it" illustrate the environmental influences, or capabilities, which students have to develop in order to stay in college. Because the interviews occurred in the second semester of the freshman year, it is assumed that these students have worked on these capabilities in order to stay in college. The theme "come to class and leave" illustrates the influence of family responsibility and family status. The theme "not expected to succeed" illustrates some of the aspects of academic difficulty, satisfaction with faculty, and interplays with the comfort level students feel within their environment (cultural affinity).

The following environmental influences were considered exogenous variables that influenced the latent variables: (a) family status—which represents parents' level of education, (b) family responsibilities—which considers obligations that may interfere with school work, (c) cultural affinity—which represents the presence of other Latinos in the college environment, (d) satisfaction with faculty—which looks at students' impression of the faculty as well as potential adult mentors, and (e) academic difficulties—which considers students' self-perception of their cognitive abilities.

Behaviors, Cognition, and Personal Influences

The theme "show me the way" most clearly illustrates that the experiences students had while in the college environment centered on relational issues. Influential mentors, advisers, faculty, friends, and/or family members encouraged them to be in college. These older peers or adult figures helped them create symbols that allowed them to envision success and thus create cognitive maps to maneuver the college system. The messages students receive from key actors in their high schools, such as teachers and counselors, about academic preparedness and university readiness shape students' self-perception of academic abilities and competence to navigate the academic rigor they will likely encounter in their first year (Martinez & Deil-Amen, 2015). A sense of self-efficacy developed in students, along with a strong high school culture, that influenced Latinx students' self-assessment of college readiness. In this study few of the students talked about that level of encouragement or a college-going culture within their high schools. Of those who did develop connections, mentors/advisers assisted them in figuring out the system and creating positive symbols for themselves. For this reason, the items previously used by Nora and colleagues (1997) for the encouragement scale were used as a proxy for the latent variable cultural and social symbolism. These items focus on family members', friends', and teachers'/advisers' support for students in college. Through this encouragement from family, peers, and mentors, students are better able to create the symbols necessary to envision their success. The latent variable academic behavior was operationally defined by the items Nora and colleagues (1997) named academic integration. These items focus on using tutors, meeting with faculty and academic advisers, and other academic behaviors that would lead to success in college. Students' ability to reflect on their environment and appreciate the importance of their educational experiences was seen as an internal commitment to the college experience. This capacity was operationally defined with a latent variable using the institutional commitment items from Nora and colleagues (1997) that focus on the level of importance the student placed on a college education and the sense of belonging that they feel.

The functioning required to persist in college was operationally defined using the intent-to-persist variable. Together these emerging issues serve as the basis for the reconfiguration of a different retention model for Latino students at urban universities that focuses on students' ability to make meaning of their experiences while in college rather than focusing on precollege attributes.

The reconfigured model conceptualizes the influences on the intent to stay in college as focusing on academic behaviors (defined by academic integration items in Nora et al., 1997), cultural/social symbolism (defined by encouragement items in Nora et al., 1997), and the influence these factors have on students' reflection of the environment (defined by institutional commitment items in Nora et al., 1997). These variables are considered together to look at the intent to persist for Latino/a students at urban universities (Figure 6.1).

Rather than focusing on academic deficiencies, this model focuses on the adaptations students are able to make in the college environment and the kinds of variables that can influence those adaptations and lead to academic success. This type of retention model seeks to identify ways Latinx students can modify their relationships rather than presume a disassociation from their culture (Rendon, Jalomo, & Nora, 2000). The model suggests how institutions can review and reconstruct their services to better serve Latinx students.

Culturally Sensitive Persistence Model for Latinx Students

Using structural equation modeling (SEM) on the survey data to test the initially conceptualized model (Figure 6.1) required what Byrne (1998) calls a two-step analysis process. It was conducted using LISREL (Jöreskog & Sörbom, 2001). First a confirmatory factor analysis (CFA) was performed to ensure that each latent variable was measured appropriately (Table 6.1). Results from the CFA indicated that several items were not contributing to the hypothesized latent variables and after theoretical consideration they were removed from the model. The items deleted were part of the academic integration scale and dealt with use of the library and use of a computer outside class. Because students were mostly commuter students and had other obligations, the use of the library was linked to spending more time physically on campus. The use of computers outside of class may have been linked to the digital divide and the fact that for some of these students a computer may be a luxury item. Several students spoke of using computer labs on campus, which they may associate as within the classroom environment.

The second step consisted of assessing the overall data-model fit of the model with the modified measurement portion from the first step in place (see Figure 6.1). Overall fit results suggested an acceptable fit between the collected data and the hypothesized model: while the Standardized Root Mean Square Residual (SRMR) = .062, Root Mean Square Error of Approximation (RMSEA) = .046 (confidence interval .041; .050) and Comparative Fit Index (CFI) = .97 indicate good overall data-model fit, while the Adjusted Goodness of Fit Index (AGFI) = .89 suggest some degree of data-model misfit. Hu and Bentler (1999) suggested that target values for acceptable fit are SRMR $\leq$ .08, RMSEA $\leq$ .05, CFI and AGFI $\geq$ .95. Byrne (1998) suggested that the RMSEA is perhaps the most informative criterion to consider. For this hypothesized model the RMSEA is .046, indicating a good fit. This would indicate that the hypothesized model using a social cognitive theory lens is a plausible explanation of the influences on the intent to persist in college for Latino urban university students. Again, this model does not test social cognitive theory; it only uses theory to inform how the variables are placed in the model.

In this initial model, family status, family responsibility, satisfaction with faculty, cultural affinity, and academic difficulty accounted for 20% (R^2 = .20) of the variance in academic integration (academic behaviors) and 42% (R^2 = .42) of the variance in encouragement (cultural and social symbolism). Furthermore, academic integration (academic behaviors) and encouragement (cultural/social symbolism) accounted for 25% (R^2 = .25) of the variability in institutional commitment (reflection). Finally, academic integration, institutional commitment, and encouragement explained 33% (R^2 = .33) of the variability in intent to persist.

In considering the direct and indirect effects (see Table 6.2), the effects of the latent variables institutional commitment, academic integration, and encouragement on the factor intent to persist were considered first. Only institutional commitment had a strong and significant (.54) direct effect on intent to persist; the effect of academic integration (.02) and encouragement (.05) on intent were not significant influences. The indirect effects from these two variables on intent to persist were stronger (due to a solid direct effect of institutional commitment on intent to persist). The indirect effect of academic integration through institutional commitment was .11 while the indirect effect of encouragement through institutional commitment was .21. The results should be interpreted using social cognitive theory, which could mean that the behaviors and symbols are not as important to intent to persist until the appropriate internal reflection occurs to consider college as an important aspect of students' life (institutional commitment).

Figure 6.1. Social cognitive retention model for Latino students at urban universities (standardized solution).

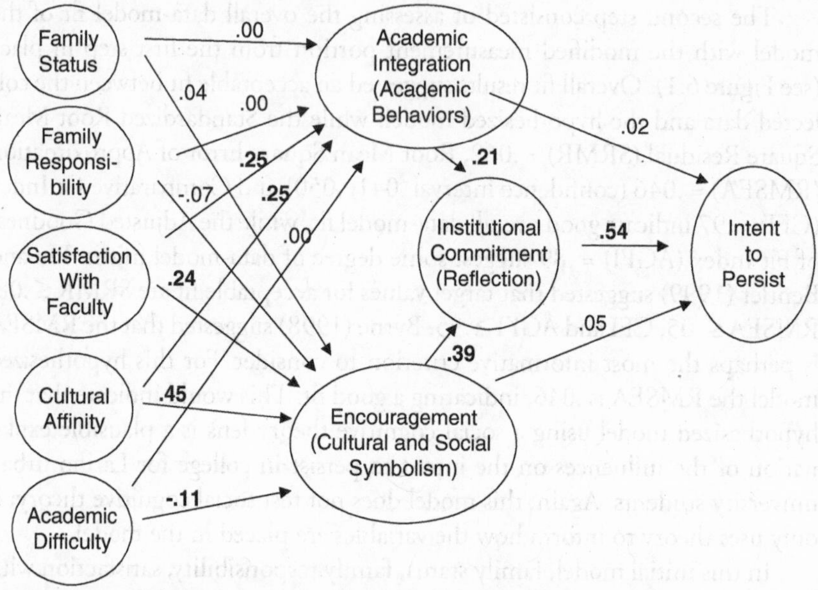

Note: Path coefficients that are bold indicate paths have a significant t-value (above 2).
Source: Torres, V. (2006). A mixed-method study testing data-model fit of a retention model for Latino/a students at urban universities. *Journal of College Student Development, 47*(3), 299–318. Reproduced with permission from ACPA College Student Education International.

TABLE 6.1
Confirmatory Factor Analysis of Items

Scale and Items	Factor Loading
Family Responsibility	
Caring for family members has made it difficult for me to study.	.50
Housework has made it difficult for me to study.	.41
Family pressures have made it difficult for me to study.	.81
Family problems have made it difficult for me to study.	.74
Encouragement	
Family members have encouraged and supported me in my decision to study.	.31
Friends have encouraged and supported me in my decision to study.	.57

Fellow students have encouraged and supported me in my decision to study.	.62
Teachers have encouraged and supported me in my decision to study.	.58
Advisors have encouraged and supported me in my decision to study.	.43
Cultural Affinity	
Latino faculty and staff help me to feel at home at this college.	.62
Other Latino students help me to feel at home at this college.	.79
Latino cultural activities help me to feel at home at this college.	.64
Satisfaction With Faculty	
I believe the instructors are well prepared for their jobs.	.47
I have good relationships with my instructors.	.47
I believe that I have learned how to study effectively.	.39
The instructions my teachers give me are clear.	.49
Academic Difficulty	
I find classes at this institution to be more difficult than I expected.	.14
I have problems understanding what I read in English.	.43
The textbooks are too hard to read.	.76
The teachers are very demanding.	.28
Institutional Commitment	
I would recommend that my friends and relatives come to this college to study.	.45
This college is important in my life.	.57
I am certain this college is the right choice for me.	.86
I feel like I belong at this college.	.73
Academic Integration	
How often do you use the library?	.11
How often do you use tutoring help?	.34
How often do you use a computer outside of class?	.005
How often do you meet with instructors outside of class?	.44
How often do you meet with your academic advisor?	.27

Source: Torres, V. (2006). A mixed method study testing data-model fit of a retention model for Latino/a students at urban universities. *Journal of College Student Development, 4*(3), 299–318. Reproduced with permission from ACPA College Student Education International.

TABLE 6.2
Direct, Indirect, and Total Effects on Endogenous Variables (Standardized Path Coefficients)

Variables [R^2]	*Direct*	*Indirect*	*Total*
On Intent to Persist [R^2 =.33]			
Institutional Commitment	.54*		
Academic Integration	.02	.11	.13
Encouragement	.02	.21	.23
On Institutional Commitment [R^2 =.25]			
Academic Integration	.21*		
Encouragement	.39*		
On Academic Integration [R^2 =.20]			
Family Status	.04		
Family Responsibility	.07		
Satisfaction With Faculty	.25*		
Cultural Affinity	.25*		
Academic Difficulty	.00		
On Encouragement [R^2 =.42]			
Family Status	.0005		
Family Responsibility	.002		
Satisfaction With Faculty	.24*		
Cultural Affinity	.45*		
Academic Difficulty	-.11*		

* Indicates significant direct effect path coefficients
Source: Torres, V. (2006). A mixed method study testing data-model fit of a retention model for Latino/a students at urban universities. *Journal of College Student Development, 47*(3), 299–318. Reproduced with permission from ACPA College Student Education International.

Finally, in considering the effects of the exogenous variables on the endogenous variables, two variables yielded interesting results. The largest influence (direct effect) on encouragement was cultural affinity (.45) followed by satisfaction with faculty (.24). The same two exogenous variables had the largest influence on academic integration with cultural affinity having a .25 direct effect and satisfaction with faculty having a .25 direct effect. The largest total effect (the sum of direct and indirect effect components) was

.715 and occurred between cultural affinity and intent to persist, through both encouragement and institutional commitment.

Summary

This model further challenges the retention theories that are dependent on looking at the institutional fit approach for commuter and underrepresented students. There is ample evidence to question if this approach explains the real situations faced by students who are economically or culturally limited to certain college choices (Rendon et al., 2000; Tierney, 1992). In addition, pointing out what students lack (the deficiency approach) focuses on the poor academic preparation received prior to attending college and does not recognize the potential in students (Tierney, 2000). What we learned from this model falls into three areas: First, the need to help students create cognitive maps that show them how to navigate the college environment; second, the role of mentoring that can help students create positive symbols; and third, the need to include social and cultural values on campus to create more inclusive space for students.

Creating Cognitive Maps

Many students in commuter urban universities are likely to be first-generation-in-college students who are not likely to have information on ways to navigate the higher education landscape. This makes helping students create cognitive maps an essential part of helping students succeed. For these Latinx students to learn the capacity to have forethought about how to succeed, they must be taught the process of creating a cognitive map that includes positive symbols, self-reflection, self-regulations, and forethought that will allow them to understand and maneuver within college processes. This is critical for Latinx students, who often have additional pressures to not only understand the college experience themselves but also explain it to their parents (Torres, 2004a).

The NSSE was used to consider colleges with higher than predicted scores on the survey to see what aspects the institution used to help underrepresented students succeed. One of the lessons learned is that colleges need to "recognize that new students need affirmation, encouragement, and support as well as information about what to do to be successful" (Whitt, 2005, p. 3). This illustrates that institutions need to see themselves as cocreators of students' cognitive maps. This model further highlights this need among Latinx commuter college students.

The role of institutional commitment was interpreted in this study as the ability to reflect on the environment and to accept the college experience as an important part of students' lives. As students create their cognitive maps on how to succeed they are better able to adjust their behavior in ways that help them succeed. Garza, Bain, and Kupczynski (2014) examined success factors on Latinx college seniors and found those who made it to their senior year of college "have learned to adapt and adjust to college life and have developed a high sense of resiliency, self-efficacy, and persistence" (p. 11). With this feeling of success comes the reflective aspect necessary to achieve a stronger level of institutional commitment and the self-regulating behaviors that promote academic success. When students understand the importance of having a college degree, they are better able to create symbols that help them conceptualize how to manage their behavior, the environment, and the personal and cognitive factors that impact their ability to succeed in college. These learning processes are the foundation of social cognitive theory (Bandura, 1986).

Role of Mentoring

Enhancing cognitive factors is one of the primary roles of mentors and advisers who help students create positive symbols "that transcend their sensory experiences" (Bandura, 1986, pg. 18). Using these symbols, students can generate innovative ways to complete their tasks and learn vicariously from their observations. The lived experiences of many urban commuter students may not allow them to make the sacrifices and devote necessary energy to be successful college students. While familial support is important for these Latinx students, they also repeatedly mentioned that although parents were supportive, they did not understand what college life was about (Torres, 2004a). This dissonance between support and understanding makes it critical to have mentors and advisers who understand the students' cultural needs as well as the college environment. Decreasing dissonance through challenge and support mechanisms allows students to gain the capacity to create their own symbols. The use of mentors in the college environment is advocated through other research (Hamrick & Stage, 2004; Torres & Hernandez, 2009) and is one of the foundational aspects of academic support programs (Torres, 2003b). A slightly different approach in academic advising is seeing the role as one-on-one coaching with a goal to change behaviors in order to improve performance.

The analysis of the total effects showed that the largest effect (the sum of direct and indirect effect components) occurred between cultural affinity and intent to persist, through both encouragement and institutional commitment. This highlighted that the presence and positive representation of Latino culture within the environment and among faculty, staff, and students is an important and significant role in students' intent to persist.

Because first-generation college students may lack the social, cultural, or economic capital needed to be successful in a college environment, it is important to enhance students' ability to create positive symbols for success. By creating positive symbols, students can transform negative or erroneous information into positive messages and better interpret their misconceptions (Bandura, 1986).

Inclusion of Cultural Values

It is critical to understand that students do not leave their cultural values at the door when they come to college. Assuming students will accept and incorporate the values within higher education is a misconception among practitioners and faculty. The focus should be on helping students create mechanisms that assist students in making the modifications to their relationships that will benefit them in the future (Rendon et al., 2000). These modifications are made gradually and are closely tied to the student's ability to conceptualize a different future that includes higher education. The challenge in creating inclusive environments is to "develop ways in which an individual's identity is affirmed, honored, and incorporated into the organizations' culture" (Tierney, 2000, p. 219). The model shows the strong direct effect cultural affinity (i.e., ability to see oneself in the culture) has on intent to persist. In order to address the challenge of creating inclusive environments, Tierney (2000) recommends that institutions look at models that address collaborative relationships dealing with power; establish connections among home, community, and schools; address issues of remediation; and provide the academic support needed for students to succeed. With this type of environment, students are better able to gain the capacities needed to have more self-efficacy and thus, succeed within the college environment. Without these enhancements Latinx students at urban commuter universities are less likely to succeed (Kuh, Kinzie, Schuh, & Whitt, 2011).

7

CRITICAL INSIGHTS FOR FUTURE RESEARCH ON LATINX IDENTITY DEVELOPMENT

The increases in the Latino population require that every practitioner and researcher understand the influences that affect Latinx students and adults. The lifespan Latinx identity development model significantly contributes to our understanding of how identity develops across the adult lifespan. It clearly shows how racism, or critical dissonance, plays a pivotal role in moving adults from being externally defined to engaging in a developmental process that does not have an end point. Instead, individuals develop the skills and strategies to work through challenges in the environment and personal changes. This model also shows how Latinos shift from exploring what it means to be Latino to making cultural commitments illustrated by taking on leadership positions or substantial long-term commitments in Latino-based organizations and serving as an advocate for the Latino community or taking on educational activities (e.g., declaring a Latino Studies major). There is no endpoint in this model, suggesting that identity development is a lifelong process. Latinos engage in a looping process that can be triggered by a new experience or environment. This then challenges individuals to revisit how they make meaning of their own Latino identity.

One of the most significant contributions of this research is the examination of the impact that the environment plays in identity development. Context may provide the trigger (critical dissonance) that makes Latinx identity salient, which then requires Latinos to make sense of who they are in response to racism, negative stereotypes, and new knowledge about identity politics or cultural history. During college, educators should support students' meaning-making process by providing them with a supportive environment where they listen to their stories, validate their feelings, and connect them with mentors to whom they feel they can relate. This model emphasizes the need to make meaning in order to develop the critical thinking skills that allow Latinx individuals to navigate the contextual and social changes that can occur throughout the lifespan.

Context also plays a significant role in future Latino identity development research. As U.S. identity politics change due to recent political events and new scholars contribute new perspectives and research approaches to the study of identity development, we look forward to continuing work that responds to these changes and creating theory that is more representative and inclusive of the broad spectrum of Latinx identities. In this final chapter, we review the continuing evolution of defining Latino identity in a way that reflects cultural and political shifts in the United States, and emerging trends in student development theory that includes critical, poststructural, and intersectional approaches. In the process, we also make recommendations for future work in understanding Latino identity development.

Troubling the Meaning and Use of "Latino" as an Ethnic Label

The meaning of *Latino* is changing as our American culture changes. One such indicator is the changing of ethnic labels that represent new perspectives about how Latino identity is defined and enacted. As stated in chapter 1, for the past few decades, the most common practice has been to use Latina/o (or Latin@) to be clearly inclusive of both men and women. Today, some individuals within the Latino community are identifying as gender fluid, nonconforming, and/or trans*, which makes the use of gendered terms problematic. In the summer of 2016, the Latina/o Knowledge Community (LKC) of NASPA–Student Affairs Administrators in Higher Education (NASPA), an association for student affairs educators, considered a name change. Members acknowledged the growing practice of using Latinx among student affairs professionals, preferring it to the use of Latina/o. The LKC voted for a name change from "Latina/o" to "Latinx/a/o." Citing that Latina and Latino are feminine and masculine respectively, the inclusion of Latinx, a gender-neutral descriptor, in the group's name, "allows for our nonbinary, genderqueer, gender fluid, and trans *hermanos* and *hermanas* to feel included." The American College Personnel Association (ACPA) College Student Educators International's counterpart to the LKC, the Latin@/x Network, also underwent a name change to be inclusive of Latinx members that same year.

According to Oboler (1995) who has researched the use of ethnic labels by Latinos (or Hispanics) in the United States, labels such as *Latino* "are proposed from a political position and used by a particular social grouping according to the particular and changing social value attributed to them within specific contexts" (p. xvi). Thus, the name changes in these college student educators' professional organizations reflect the changing political and cultural norms in the United States. The Latinx ethnic identity label first appeared in 2014 on the Internet and social media sites. College students began to use it for personal self-identification and to rename their organizations to clearly indicate a more inclusive, socially aware attitude. *Latinx* as a term then began to appear in more professional areas of higher education, such as published, peer-reviewed scholarly articles and professional conferences (Salinas & Lozano, 2017). Although the use of *Latinx* has increased every year, there are some arguments against its use. Namely, some assert that the term is only a buzzword predominantly used in the United States and that its use cannot be considered "speaking Spanish" (Guerrera & Orbea, 2015, as cited in Salinas & Lozano, 2017, p. 5).

Salinas and Lozano (2017) challenge educators to share their own positionality and reflexivity on the term *Latinx*, and we do so here by asking: What could this increasing use of Latinx mean for our scholarship in Latino identity development? First, we questioned whether we should have followed suit and used the term *Latinx* in this book. We were hesitant at times, and as native Spanish speakers we could see both sides of this issue. Our prior work used the terms *Latina/o* when talking about individual development; equally importantly, none of the students in our study identified as Latinx, mainly because it was not common to identify as such when we conducted the interviews and collected surveys. Second, we were challenged to consider shifting away from a binary perspective. Doing so is not only inclusive but reflects the ways that people are currently identifying and should be considered in our future identity development research. In the end we used the term *Latinx* when referencing individuals but continued the use of terms *Latino culture* or *Latino/a* when speaking about the known gender of the participant.

The issue of language and terms is of continuing concern for any researcher or practitioner working on issues of identity. Although we asked participants to self-identify their ethnicity and they responded with varying detail about their choice of ethnic label, future research could include asking participants how they make meaning of other ethnic labels that could apply, such as Chicana/o, Boricua, Afro Latina/o, or Latinx. Such questions might reveal additional cultural nuances between different cultural groups and the role that context might play in the use of certain labels.

The Impact of Politics on Latino Identity

The ways that individuals make meaning of and express their Latino identity are strongly shaped by the prevailing American political climate. Over the decades, the spectrum of Latino identities has ranged from "wanting to be White" assimilationist to possessing and showcasing strong ethnocentric pride. For example, during the Great Depression Latinos feared deportation due to mass repatriation drives. As a result, they largely advocated for assimilation by downplaying their Latino roots, limiting their use of the Spanish language, and emphasizing their American citizenship as a means of protection (Gutierrez, 1995). This sense of Latino identity was in sharp contrast to the ethnocentric Brown Pride in the 1960s and 1970s that rejected assimilation, embraced militant activism, and showed pride in indigenous roots (Gutierrez, 1995).

At the time of this publication, it is difficult to not acknowledge the current political climate created by the Trump administration. It is especially hostile for Latinos, a result of derogatory public statements about Latinos, a promise to build a wall between Mexico and the United States, and the decision to phase out the Deferred Action for Childhood Arrivals (DACA) program (Duke, 2017). These new political realities, in addition to increasing numbers of hate crimes on campuses and rising xenophobia (Dreid & Najmabadi, 2016), can result in Latinx students feeling marginalized, targeted, and unsafe. Prior research has demonstrated the impact of political realities, discriminatory policies, and institutionalized racism on Latinos' holistic development (Hernández, 2012; Torres, 2009; Torres & Baxter Magolda, 2004). Often, racism results in individuals experiencing critical dissonance, which then may result in being pushed to make meaning of that racist incident and the significance that being a racial/ethnic minority has in their lives. However, this level of overt hostility is now at a substantially higher level. Prior research has shown that experiencing significant dissonance without the appropriate level of support to work through it may result in developmental regression (Torres & Hernandez, 2007). As a result, the heightened and prolonged levels of racism, White supremacy activism, and anti-immigrant sentiment experienced during this political era may be overwhelming and substantially detrimental for many Latinx students who do not have the support and resources to deal with these circumstances. Many U.S. citizens consider all Latinos to be the same and therefore these attitudes impact all of us, regardless of immigration status. Future studies in Latino identity development might illustrate how individuals make meaning of what it means to be Latino as anti-Latino policies or sentiments in the political sphere ebb and flow.

Disentangling Ethnic Identity From Racial Identity

The term *Latino* has been used as both a racial category and ethnic identity. For Latinos, our ethnic identity generally refers to our national origins (e.g., Mexican, Puerto Rican, or Peruvian) and can be a source of cultural pride and sense of belonging to a cultural community (Johnston-Guerrero, 2016). Defining our race is more challenging; some Latinos might not distinguish between racial and ethnic identity. Adding to the confusion are the census racial categories that require individuals to select their ethnicity (Hispanic or non-Hispanic) and then their race (White, Black, Asian/Pacific Islander, or American Indian/Alaskan Native), which can be troubling if individuals only identify with their ethnicity and not a racial category or have varying conceptualizations of what these racial categories mean (Strmic-Pawl, Jackson, & Garner, 2017. The term *Mestizo* is also used to represent the mixing of multiple races within Latino history (European, Indigenous, African, or others). There is no general consensus on a singular racial identity for Latinos; "many Latinos/as racially identify as White, Black, or other, but culturally identify as Latino/as or with their national origin" (Golash-Boza & Darity, 2008, p. 907).

Recent Latino research has placed race as a central focus by investigating the experiences of Afro Latinos in college. This emerging body of research challenges the practice of conflating Latino as both an ethnicity and racial category by clearly differentiating Latino as an ethnicity and Black as a racial category. The research acknowledges the historical legacy of negating or making invisible African roots in Latino communities and challenges scholarship on Latino college students that has practically rendered Afro Latinos invisible, while at the same time norming Latino identity to be largely based on Mexican American, Mestizo culture. This line of research also reveals the anti-Black racism in the Latino community and the ways that Latinos ascribe toward Whiteness by downplaying or negating African roots and privileging lighter skinned Latinos, all of which may contribute to Afro Latinos feeling marginalized and discriminated against within their own Latino communities (Haywood, 2017). Afro Latinos constantly have to deal with a sense of foreignness in their own communities, where their identities are assumed to be Anglo Black and not authentic Latina/os (Hernández, 2003).

Haywood (2017) recommends that scholars who study Latino identity should disentangle race and ethnicity and also consider how the body (phenotype, hair, and other features that might suggest being identified with a particular racial category) could affect how Latinos make meaning of their ethnic identity. Colorism, anti-Black racism, and marginalization within the Latino community may affect how Afro Latinos make meaning of their own identity in unique ways that their other Latino peers may not experience. Haywood also recommends that scholars collect demographic data that include both race and ethnicity to make visible the racial composition of one's sample, focus on intragroup dynamics along racial lines, and recognize how context (e.g., institutional type or diversity mix in student population) might influence meaning-making of identities.

Critical Perspectives in Identity Development Research

The use of critical and poststructural theories in student development scholarship is becoming more prevalent, including studies that focus on Latina/o development. These studies have resulted in new insights about the ways that power, privilege, and oppression might influence individuals' lived experiences, which then affects how they make meaning of their identities. Critical theories provide concepts and language that can be useful tools for digging into the messiness of examining these connections between social forces and identity sense-making and share the same "purpose of inquiry to promote fundamental social change by raising consciousness and correcting injustices" (Patton, Renn, Guido, & Quaye, 2016, p. 25). In other words, critical theories do not tell us how identity shifts in complexity over time, or how individuals make meaning of identity; rather they provide different lenses to view and make meaning of identity development.

Jones and Stewart (2016) reviewed the evolution of student development theory scholarship and depicted three waves of student development theory scholarship. These waves indicate the changing perspectives of how we conceptualize development, what we consider to be important in the investigation of development, and the student voices that are represented in these theories. The first wave included foundational theories that tended to be based on positivistic epistemology and White, privileged male samples. The second wave was research that was grounded in constructivist epistemology that included minoritized populations. The third wave included critical and poststructural theories (e.g., critical race theory [CRT], queer theory, intersectionality, and feminism) to understand how power, oppression, and social context might influence the development for both privileged and marginalized identities.

Identity development research is currently in the middle of overlapping waves. Researchers studying Latino identity development are working from second and/or third wave approaches to development. Research that contributed to the development of the lifespan Latinx identity development model began at a time when the use of critical theories was not as common. As a result, this research used a constructivist epistemological stance, which places this work within the traditions of the second wave of student development. We placed the students' voices at the center of understanding the meaning-making process, and we recognize that this approach both helps and hinders our understanding of Latino identity development. While these narratives certainly included stories that illustrated how participants made meaning of racism and negative stereotypes about Latinos, this research project did not begin with a focus primarily on how power, privilege, and oppression might affect development, and therefore it was not appropriate to apply this lens in retrospect. On one hand, our constructivist approach can be viewed as a strength, as these issues emerged on their own, which makes the findings more powerful. However, on the other hand, not making racism a central focus might have produced more opportunities for students to voice their understanding of these social forces.

Third wave scholarship has yielded new insights to the study of Latino identity and complicates further the ways that context influences development. In the following, critical and poststructural approaches are reviewed and then compared to this work, showing the strengths and limitations of each.

CRT

CRT is definitively placed in the third wave of developmental scholarship. CRT, which places race and ethnicity at the center of the study of the student experience (Solórzano, 1998), has been a useful theoretical framework to understand Latinx students' racialized realities. CRT scholarship in education includes five elements: the centrality of race and racism, challenges to dominant ideologies such as meritocracy and equal opportunity, a commitment to social justice, the centrality of experiential knowledge, and placing research within a historical context and an interdisciplinary perspective (Solórzano, 1998). While more and more higher education scholars are using CRT in their work, CRT in student development research is still relatively new. Ebelia Hernández applied CRT to her work on Mexican American women activists' holistic development, which revealed new elements to consider in the study of identity development (Hernández, 2016). For example, her work connected how these women's development of political consciousness led to higher levels of internalized motivation to advocate for the Latino community (Hernández, 2012). The more they knew about the injustices their community faced, such as racist legislation and policies, the more they internalized a sense of obligation to serve their community to resist these injustices, which in turn became a part of how they lived out their Latina identities. This development of an internalized motivation to advocate for the Latino community corresponds with the lifespan Latinx identity development model in demonstrating the process toward internalized identity/enacted commitments where individuals take on leadership positions to indicate their commitment to serve their communities.

Research that incorporates CRT in the study of ethnic identity of marginalized people of color examines the extent to which racism affects development, as well as the process of developing critical consciousness. These central foci complement the findings from this book as well as findings from our prior studies that also revealed the developmental tasks of making meaning of racism (Torres, 2009). The findings were similar, but using a CRT theoretical perspective requires questions be asked about race, ethnicity, and experiences with oppression, whereas non-CRT studies might allow for these topics to emerge organically from the participants. The advantage of using CRT is that it allows for a more complex understanding of racism, but a disadvantage might be that not all Latinos consider their race and ethnic identities to be central to their lived experiences. As a result, using such a framework may not provide full opportunity to examine other forms of oppression, such as homophobia and sexism.

Intersectionality

Poststructural theories, such as intersectionality and queer theory, recognize that individuals hold multiple, intersecting identities that influence each other. In addition, poststructural theories consider identity to be a fluid, ever-changing process of meaning-making and performance that is informed by context, thus making it difficult and undesirable to constrain such a fluid process in a model, particularly one that is linear or suggests a trajectory from being externally defined to an internalized sense of self (Jones, 2009). Developmental scholarship that uses intersectionality does not just examine multiple identities; it applies a theoretical approach that includes examining multiple identities to investiage how privilege and marginalization function in our society (Dill & Zambrana, 2009). Intersectional research includes four tenets:

1. Centering the study on the lived experiences of marginalized people
2. Recognizing that identity is both individual and group
3. Exploring of identity salience and how it is influenced by social forces, such as power, privilege, and inequality
4. Creating and maintaining a social justice agenda (Dill & Zambrana, 2009).

Jones' (2009, 2010) intersectional work illustrated how individuals make meaning of social forces and manage their multiple identities in response to these contextual factors. Using an autoethnographic approach, Jones has examined how individuals manage and make meaning of their privileged and marginalized identities. The most significant finding from this work was recognizing how "the individual both acts on and is acted upon by context" (Jones, 2009, p. 301). Individuals *act on* context by manipulating the identities they present based on context, perhaps by emphasizing their privileged identities and diminishing or making invisible their marginalized identities. For example, a Latina woman might have the agency to emphasize her ethnic identity to seek out community in a group of Latinos and diminish or hide her undocumented status if she is unsure of the group's stance toward immigration. Individuals are *acted upon* by acts of racism and oppression that they cannot control but are the result of their marginalized identities. To continue the previous example, the Latina woman endures anti-immigrant comments in her class, as well as policies that threaten her DACA status.

The benefit of using intersectionality as a theoretical perspective in identity development research is that it fully acknowledges that people are a compilation of multiple identities that influence each other in unique ways. Intersectionality may be particularly useful for studies that investigate race and ethnicity (Afro Latinos) or ethnicity and gender (Latinx).

Similar to Anzaldúa's (1999) work in which she made meaning of her own multiple identities as a Chicana lesbian living in the borderlands, we can investigate how ethnic, gender, and sexual identities clash, complement, and challenge each other by using intersectionality. The concept of borderlands was useful in understanding the complex construction of identity among the participants in these studies and the development of the lifespan Latinx identity development model, yet intersectionality was not foregrounded in these studies. This is where our use of constructivist epistemology that focuses on the emergent of issues may have been a limitation. At the same time, like issues advocated through a CRT lens, these issues did emerge and thus verified the need to consider the use of these lenses in research.

In summary, this chapter considers new theoretical directions in identity development research, critiques our own research design, and provides exciting new directions and ways to conceptualize identity. In particular, we advocate for additional research that interrogates terms used to identify the Latino population, explores the impact of political sentiments about the Latino population on identity development, and disentangles race and ethnicity. Further, in this review of research that uses CRT and intersectionality as theoretical perspectives, we are recognizing the impact that social forces have on identity development. This third wave of developmental scholarship should be viewed as research complementary to second wave scholarship. Second wave scholarship as represented by our work places the student voice at the center, which we find of great value, but third wave scholarship explicitly interrogates systems of oppression, which may be lost with a constructivist approach. Each wave contributes to our understanding of the impact of racism in identity development in different ways, providing both advantages and limitations. The lifespan Latinx identity development model is a contribution to our understanding of the ways that racism impacts development, specifically the finding that critical dissonance is a significant developmental experience that propels individuals toward examining the meaning of their Latino identity. Because they are complementary, research that combines elements of both second and third wave approaches to developmental research is not only possible, but has been done. An example is Hernández's (2006) research that employed a social constructionist perspective (second wave) and CRT (third wave), which centered the participants' voices to understand their racialized experiences. Future research from both constructivist and critical perspectives will continue to investigate the impact of racism and other forms of oppression on Latino identity development.

Like all research, what was investigated previously only informs future research to consider issues in a more in-depth manner. The longitudinal nature of this research promotes a longer view of how Latinx students navigate their identity and their college experience. The difficult questions that need to be considered in the future would benefit greatly from other longitudinal designs that value processes, not just outcomes. As third wave research becomes the norm, considering the influence of power and oppression on the longitudinal nature of development will be important to consider. Like many research projects, we leave future researchers to consider all the gaps in this study.

APPENDIX A

DEFINING THE TERMS USED BY LATINOS

There are multiple terms used to describe the individuals whose countries of origin are Spanish speaking. Following is a brief description of various terms by which Latinos choose to identify.

Hispanic

The term *Hispanic* was developed by the U.S. government in the 1970s, specifically by the U.S. Census, to begin counting the Spanish-speaking population in the United States (Nelson & Tienda, 1997; Oboler, 1995). As a panethnic term, it implies that various Latino ethnic groups such as Mexicans/Mexican Americans, Puerto Ricans, and Cuban/Cuban Americans are culturally similar. However, Latino ethnic identity scholars have long noted that the term *Hispanic* was developed by external political forces to imply cultural similarity and cohesion when in fact the Hispanic population encompasses population groups with very different histories of U.S. incorporation (Calderón, 1992; Nelson & Tienda, 1997; Oboler, 1992; Oboler, 1995). Some groups, such as Mexicans and Mexican Americans, consist of colonized natives of the United States and their subsequent offspring, while others, such as Cubans and Cuban Americans, entered the United States as political refugees. Furthermore, the term obfuscates the diversity of the Latino population with respect to race, ethnicity, social class, immigrant status, and generation status (Gimenez, 1989; Zavella, 1991). Despite the problematic nature of the term *Hispanic* as outlined by Latino ethnic identity scholars, it is the term the U.S. government continues to employ when reporting economic, educational, and family trends. In addition, it is a term that many Latinos in the United States prefer over others.

Latino

Scholars are not the only individuals to take issues with the term *Hispanic*. Some Latinos themselves have rejected the term because it overemphasizes the European or Spanish heritage of the population while ignoring its indigenous roots. In addition, noting that Hispanic is a socially constructed category for the reasons mentioned previously, Chicano and Puerto Rican activists in the 1970s preferred the term *Latino* to unite Latino ethnic groups in their struggles for economic, political, and educational opportunities during the civil rights movement (Calderón, 1992). Recent polls show that most Hispanics or Latinos have no preference for a particular term (Pew Research Center, 2013). Fifty percent of Hispanics/Latinos have no preference for either "Hispanic" or "Latino." About a third prefer "Hispanic," and only 15% prefer "Latino." Not surprisingly, the 2013 poll does show some regional differences. In Texas, close to half of the Latino population prefers "Hispanic." Other scholars have noted the preference for "Hispanic" in the Southwest in comparison to other parts of the country (Gimenez, 1989; Zavella, 1991).

Chicano

The term *Chicano* specifically refers to Mexican Americans, particularly those from the West Coast. The label became popular with Mexican Americans during the 1960s when they fought to reject categories such as Hispanic and Spanish American, which many Chicano movement leaders felt implied assimilation of Latino population groups into U.S. society (Calderon, 1992). Wanting to highlight their Indian or indigenous roots, Mexican Americans on the West Coast embraced the term *Chicano*. Since the term originated during the civil rights movement, it connotes some level of militancy and political activism. As a result, Mexican Americans in the United States do not unilaterally embrace the term.

Specific Country of Origin

While half of Latinos or Hispanics report no preference between "Hispanic" or "Latino" (Pew Research Center, 2013), when asked how they most often describe themselves, the majority of Latinos appear to prefer to identify using their country of origin. On average, 54% of Latinos describe themselves using their specific country of origin. Dominicans are the most likely at 66%, then Cubans at 63%, and Salvadorans are the least likely at 49% (Pew Research Center, 2013). The preference for use of a specific country of origin among Latinos is surprising and interesting since the majority of Latinos are born in the United States. About 35% of the Latino population was born outside of the United States (Krogstad & Lopez, 2014). However, if we once again highlight the ethnic diversity of the Latino population in the United States, it is perhaps not so surprising to find that Latinos prefer to identify with their specific country of origin. The preference for the use of their specific country of origin may also be a way for particular Latino ethnic groups such as Dominicans and Cubans to distinguish themselves from the largest Latino ethnic population in the United States, Mexicans and Mexican Americans, which comprise more than two-thirds of the Latino population.

Puerto Ricans/Nuyoricans

While the majority of Latinos are born in the United States, only 23% prefer to describe themselves as "American." Salvadorans are the least likely to describe themselves as "American" (12%), while Puerto Ricans are the most likely to do so at 28%. Since Puerto Rico is a U.S. territory, Puerto Ricans are U.S. citizens, which could explain their preference for the label "American" in comparison to other Latino ethnic groups. Furthermore, because Puerto Ricans primarily settled on the East Coast, specifically New York during the 1940s through the 1960s, subsequent Puerto Rican generations born and raised in New York have also embraced the term *Nuyorican* (Nelson & Tienda, 1997). As Nelson and Tienda (1997) write, the term indicates "a simultaneous separateness from Puerto Rico and their connection to it" (p. 14).

Latinx

The term *Latinx* (pronounced La-teen-ex) has become a popular alternative to both Latino and Latina. Its use gained traction among queer communities rejecting the gender binary imposed by the use of Latino/a, Latina/o, or Latin@. Advocates embrace how the term advances social justice for queer and non-gender-conforming individuals. Critics note it is another form of linguistic imperialism; specifically, U.S.-born Latinos imposing new language on predominantly Spanish-speaking Latinos who may struggle to use or pronounce the term *Latinx* (see de Onis, 2017 for debate).

Summary

Overall, while use of the terms *Hispanic* and *Latino* permeates throughout the media and even academic scholarship, the representative data presented in this appendix clearly show that Latinos in the United States choose a variety of terms when describing how they identify. Identity is highly subjective and context driven. In other words, in some situations, Latinos may embrace panethnic terms but in others, a specific country of origin term is preferred.

APPENDIX B

METHODOLOGY FOR LONGITUDINAL STUDY

Investigating the Complexities of the Choice to Stay in College for Latino Students

Field Initiated Study grant from the U.S. Department of Education (R 305T010160).

Human Subjects Approvals:
George Washington University: U020104
Indiana University: 03-8436

Research Questions

- Do the characteristics previously determined to predict persistence also predict Latino student retention? What other characteristics promote persistence among Latino students?
- How does the college experience affect Latino students' cultural orientation and their choice to stay in college? And how does Latino students' cultural orientation affect their college experience and their choice to stay in college?
- Do Latino students in diverse types of higher education institutions differ? If so, how do environmental factors influence their choice to stay in college?

Methodology

This project was a multi-institutional, mixed-methods longitudinal design that utilized a constructivist epistemology, which recognizes that the interaction between researcher and participants is an important aspect to understanding the meaning of experiences shared during the research process (Lincoln & Guba, 1985; Charmaz, 2000). The use of both qualitative and quantitative methods in this study required that the methodology include multiple methods. Grounded theory methodology was selected for two important reasons. First, the goal of the research was to understand the emerging theory to provide a plausible explanation of the phenomenon by grounding the theory in the data (Strauss & Corbin, 1998). Through constructivist grounded theory the "'discovered' reality arises from the interactive process" between participant and researcher (Charmaz, 2000, p. 524). The second reason acknowledges that both qualitative and quantitative methods "have roles to play in theorizing" (Strauss & Corbin, 1998, p. 34) and the grounded theory research process. The key to using mixed methods is to have a circular interplay where the qualitative data direct the quantitative data and then feed back to inform the qualitative data. This circular process is also an evolving process where each method is contributing to the theory in ways that are unique to the method considered. The use of grounded theory methodology requires concepts to emerge from the data; therefore, the qualitative method was given priority. This research decision to give one method priority supports the concurrent nested strategy design used in this study (Creswell, 2003; Strauss & Corbin, 1998).

Research Design

All entering Latino freshmen at seven institutions were asked to participate in this study [design was changed to three urban universities in the second year]. Participants were followed for the four or more years they were in college (even though this follow-up may extend beyond the framework of this requested funding). A mixed-methods approach was used to investigate the research questions so as to understand the complex issues surrounding the choice to stay in college. Each year data were collected through surveys and in-depth interviews. Survey-only participants received annual follow-up surveys to enhance this project's understanding of the longitudinal effects of the quantitative variables.

The guidelines of grounded theory methodology (Strauss & Corbin, 1998) frame this study. Grounded theory allows for constant comparison within the qualitative data and with the quantitative measures, while maintaining a central focus on the development or creation of theory. This methodology was chosen because it focuses on the grounding of theory in data, and it allows for the elaboration or modification of existing theories by constantly comparing these assumptions with the new data collected. Verification of assumptions were done throughout the research project and not left to a further study. The following sections will elaborate on the methods used to explore the complexity of assumptions found in the literature in greater depth.

Sample

Qualitative and quantitative data were obtained from 3 urban institutions, and only qualitative interviews were collected from a fourth urban university. Two of the institutions are Hispanic-serving institutions (HSIs); one with over 90% Latinx student enrollment and the other with approximately 28% Latino/a representation. The other 2 institutions represent a predominantly White environment (with Latinx students representing approximately 4% of the overall undergraduate population).

For the survey portion all self-identified Latinx freshmen at the participating urban universities were surveyed in the spring of 2003 (N = 1474). The response rate was 36.7% (n = 541) and approximately 6.3% of the students that responded to the survey were interviewed within their own university environment.

The sample of students who responded to the survey included more females (64%) and a mean age of 20.73 (SD = 5.8). Most of the students were born in the United States to parents who are immigrants (labeled as second generation in the United States, 59%), while only 18.4% (100) were foreign-born. The remaining students were third generation or beyond in the United States. Approximately 77% of the students are first-generation college students, and the majority claim Mexico as their country of origin, followed by Puerto Rico, Cuba, El Salvador, and other countries. The majority of students live with their parents (74.4%) and an additional 19.7% live in their own home. It is difficult to determine if this sample is representative of the overall sample at these institutions because institutions collect data on ethnicity and no other demographic characteristics. This sample does reflect characteristics of the broader Latino/a population in higher education. In the overall population the largest percentages of students are from Mexican origins (Guzman, 2000; Therrien & Ramirez, 2000) and the largest increase in college attendance is for Latinas (females of Latino origin) (American Council on Education, 2002).

An open sampling technique was used to invite participants for the interviews because the technique would not prematurely close off the sample, and the students were volunteers from the survey respondents.

The interviews took between 20 to 60 minutes, and all interviews were taped and transcribed. The content of the interviews concentrated on questions about the college environment, cultural orientation, and family influences. Additional follow-up probes were done to further prompt students to explain influences or decision-making processes about the choice to stay in school.

The interview participants were Mexican American, Puerto Rican, Cuban, El Salvadorian, Dominican, and Costa Rican. As with the survey sample, many of the interview participants were second generation in the United States, the second group were third generation and beyond in the United States, and smallest portion were born outside the United States. Each student was asked to create a pseudonym for the purpose of this study.

Survey

The survey for this study was developed to include items addressing the three areas found to be important in prior studies. The first section covers the precollege attributes, mostly demographic in nature.

The second section focuses on environmental interactions and was investigated using several lenses. Because Nora and Cabrera (1996) and Nora, Kraemer, and Itzen (1997) considered ethnicity as one of their precollege factors, the scales used by their studies were used for this study. The use of these survey items assisted in triangulating the previous findings. The scales included were campus climate (Cronbach Alpha = .83), prejudiced attitudes of faculty and staff (Cronbach Alpha = .85), encouragement (Cronbach Alpha = .78) and informal interactions with faculty and staff (Cronbach Alpha = .84).

The third section of the survey focused on the choices students make about their culture of origin and were viewed through the lens of the bicultural orientation model (BOM) (Torres, 1999). The BOM was created by intersecting measures of acculturation and ethnic identity such that four quadrants are created. A person with a high level of acculturation and ethnic identity would be in the bicultural orientation quadrant. A person with a high level of acculturation and a low level of ethnic identity would be in the Anglo orientation. A person with a low level of acculturation and a high level of ethnic identity would be in the Hispanic orientation quadrant. And finally, a person with both a low level of acculturation and a low level of ethnic identity would be in the marginal orientation quadrant. This last classification suggests a certain level of uneasiness with both the Anglo and Hispanic cultures. The BOM allows for an individual snapshot of the choices the student has made between the Latino and Anglo culture by placing them in one of the four cultural orientations (bicultural, Anglo, Latino, or marginal orientations).

The scales used in this model include an acculturation scale (Marin, Sabogal, Marin, Otero-Sabogal, & Perez-Stable, 1987) and an ethnic identity scale (Phinney, 1992). The students' cultural orientations are determined by plotting their scores on the Short Acculturation Scale for Hispanics (Marin et al., 1987) which consists of 12 items and provides an overall score

And finally the fourth section goal commitment was investigated through three survey items comprising the goal commitment/degree completion scale (Nora & Cabrera, 1996). This allowed the researchers to understand the process involved in educational commitment.

Other items were added to the survey as they emerged in the qualitative interviews. These items included having an identified mentor or adviser and items measuring cultural conflict.

Interviews

Semistructured interviews were conducted with students from a stratified sample of each institution. Every effort was made to include the representation by culture of origin, prior academic ability, and other demographic characteristics of interest.

The interview drew out examples of students' experiences and how their cultural self-identification influenced their college experience. The interview questions focused on 3 areas: cultural self-identification, external influences on the student, and the college experience. The protocol for the interview was tested through the pilot study and is included at the end of the methodology. The interviews lasted between 20 to 60 minutes and were recorded and later transcribed.

Analysis and Trustworthiness

Analysis for the interview data was done using grounded theory techniques (Strauss & Corbin, 1998). First, open coding was used by conducting a line-by-line review of the data by the primary researcher (first author) and two inquiry auditors. Once this stage of the analysis was completed, the research team moved into axial coding thus reconnecting the pieces of the data back together into themes that could illustrate an understanding of the environmental issues being considered (Strauss & Corbin, 1998).

Trustworthiness was achieved using a variety of strategies. These strategies provide insight into the goodness (validity) of the qualitative research process (Armenio & Hultgren, 2002; Lincoln & Guba, 1985). First, a researcher's journal was maintained for reflection and to chronicle research decisions. Second, inquiry auditors were used to help the researchers interpret the data and to assist identifying potential bias or misinterpretation. And finally, because this was part of a longitudinal study, member checks were done with the participants the following year in order to ascertain if the emerging themes were appropriate assessments of their experiences.

Protocol for First-Year Interview

Introduction: This interview will focus on your experiences as a college student who has identified as Hispanic on college records. I will ask you some questions that do not have one correct answer; my goal is to understand you. The interview should not take any longer than 45 minutes and you can stop it at any time. (recording)

1. Tell me about yourself.
2. When someone says "What are you?" how do you identify yourself? (Follow-up: If ethnicity is not addressed, ask "Are there other ways you identify?")
3. What does that identification mean to you? (refer to the self-identification used in number 2)
4. Has your family influenced who you are? How?
5. Have you had any experiences that have influenced how you identify yourself? (Probes: parents' view of ethnicity, messages sent to you as a child, ethnic make-up of the area where you grew up, etc.)
6. How has being in college influenced how you see your self-identification?
7. Goals—how do you plan to achieve them?
8. Are there particular things in the college environment that have contributed to your self-identification?
9. Is there anything that you feel is relevant that I have not asked about?

Protocol for Second-Year Interview

1. How have things changed for you since the last time we talked?
2. Last year you identified yourself as [fill in according to previous interview], has that changed?
3. What are the positive and negative aspects of the environment at [institution]?

4. What issues do you see yourself dealing with this year? Possible probes: Family, choice of major, grades.
5. Specific issues about the student (conflicts previously identified; decisions about school; process for making decisions; issues about staying in school or transferring).

Protocol for Third-Year Interview

1. How have things changed for you since the last time we talked?
2. What kinds of issues do you have to deal with at this point in your college career?
3. What are the positive and negative aspects of the environment at [institution]?
   a. What do you wish you had known about the college prior to starting?
   b. What has made a difference for you?
4. What issues do you see yourself dealing with this year?
   a. Possible probes: Family, choice of major, grades.
5. Specific issues about the student (conflicts previously identified; decisions about school; process for making decisions; issues about staying in school or transferring).

Protocol for Fourth-Year Interview

1. How are things going for you?
2. How have things changed since the last time we talked?
   a. Probe for process on decision-making
3. Cultural identification—Is there something that is making a difference for you?
4. When do you think you will graduate?
5. What do you see as challenges for you at this point?
6. Are there things/programs that would help you at this point?
7. Specific issues about the student.

Protocol for Fifth-Year Interview

1. How are things going for you?
2. How have things changed since the last time we talked?
   - Probe for process on decision-making.
3. Cultural identification—Is there something that is making a difference for you?

4. Did you think you will graduate? When do you think you will graduate?
5. What do you see as challenges for you at this point?
6. Are there things/programs that would help you at this point?
7. Specific issues dealing with the student.

REFERENCES

Abes, E. S., & Jones, S. R. (2004). Meaning-making capacity and the dynamics of lesbian college students' multiple dimensions of identity. *Journal of College Student Development, 45*(6), 612–632.

Abes, E. S. & Kasch, D. (2007). Using queer theory to explore lesbian college students' multiple dimensions of identity. *Journal of College Student Development, 48*(6), 619–636.

American Council on Education (2002). *Nineteenth annual report on minorities in higher education.* Washington DC: Author.

Anzaldúa, G. (1999). *Borderlands/La frontera: The new mestiza* (2nd ed.). San Francisco, CA: Aunt Lute Books.

Arminio, J. L. and Hultgren, F. H. (2002). Breaking out from the shadow: The question of criteria in qualitative research. *Journal of College Student Development, 43*(4), 446–460.

Baxter Magolda, M. B. (1992). *Knowing and reasoning in college: Gender-related patterns in students' intellectual development.* San Francisco, CA: Jossey-Bass Publishers.

Baxter Magolda, M. B. (2001). *Making their own way: Narratives for transforming higher education to promote self-development.* Sterling, VA: Stylus.

Baxter Magolda, M. B. (2005). Complex lives. In M. E. Wilson & L. E. Wolf-Wendel (Eds.), *ASHE reader on college student development theory* (pp. 81–100). Boston, MA: Pearson.

Bandura, A. (1986). *Social foundations of thought and action: A social cognitive theory.* Englewood Cliffs, NJ: Prentice Hall.

Bean, J. P. & Metzner, B. S. (1985). A conceptual model of nontraditional undergraduate student attrition. *Review of Educational Research, 55,* 485–540.

Belenky, M. F., Clinchy, B. M., Goldberger, N. R., & Tarule, J. M. (1986). *Women's ways of knowing: The development of self, voice, and mind.* New York, NY: Basic Books.

Berry, J. W. (1994). An ecological perspective on cultural and ethnic psychology. In E. J. Trickett, R. J. Watts, and D. Birman (Eds.), *Human diversity: Perspectives on people in context* (pp. 115–141). San Francisco, CA: Jossey-Bass.

Berry, J. W., Phinney, J. S., Sam, D. L., & Vedder, P. (2006). Immigrant youth: Acculturation, identity, and adaptation. *Applied Psychology: An International Review, 55*(3), 303–332.

Bowman, N. A. (2011). Promoting participation in a diverse democracy: A meta-analysis of college diversity experiences and civic engagement. *Review of Educational Research, 81*(1), 29–68.

Bowman, N. A. (2012). Structural diversity and close interracial relationships in college. *Educational Researcher, 1*(4), 133–135.

Braxton, J. M., Doyle, W. R., Hartley III, H. V., Hirschy, A. S., Jones, W. A. & McLendon, M. K. (2014). *Rethinking college student retention*. San Francisco, CA: Jossey-Bass.

Braxton, J. M., Hirschy, A. S. & McClendon, S. A. (2004). Understanding and reducing college student departure. *ASHE-ERIC Higher Education Report, 30*(3). San Francisco, CA: Jossey-Bass.

Byrne, B. M. (1998). *Structural equation modeling with LISREL, PRELIS, and SIMPLIS: Basic concepts, applications, and programming*. Mahwah, NJ: Erlbaum

Calderón, J. (1992). "Hispanic" and "Latino": The viability of categories for panethnic unity. *Latin American Perspectives, 19*, 37–44.

Charmaz, K. (2000). Grounded theory objectivist and constructivist methods. In N. K. Denzin and Y. S. Lincoln (Eds.) *Handbook of Qualitative Research* (2nd ed.) (pp. 509–536). Thousand Oaks, CA: Sage.

Chavez, L. (2008). *The Latino threat: Constructing immigrants, citizens, and the nation.* Stanford, CA: Stanford University Press.

Contreras, F. E., Malcom, L. E., & Bensimon, E. M. (2008). Hispanic-serving institutions: Closeted identity and the production of equitable outcomes for Latino/a students. In M. Gasman, B. Baez, & C. S. V. Turner (Eds.), *Understanding minority-serving institutions* (pp. 71–90). Albany, NY: State University of New York Press.

Creswell, J. W. (2003). *Research design qualitative, quantitative, and mixed methods approaches*, (2nd ed.). Thousand Oaks, CA: Sage.

Creswell, J. W. & Plano Clark, V. L. (2007). *Designing and conducting mixed methods research*. Thousand Oaks, CA: Sage.

Crocker, L. & Algina, J. (1986). *Introduction to classical & modern test theory*. Orlando, FL: Harcourt Brace Jovanovich College Publishers.

Cross, W. E. (1995). The psychology of nigrescence: Revising the Cross model. In J. G. Ponterotto, J. M. Casas, L. A. Suzuki, and C. M. Alexander (Eds.), *Handbook of multicultural counseling* (pp. 93–122). Thousand Oaks, CA: Sage.

Cuellar, M. (2015). Latina/o student characteristics and outcomes at four-year Hispanic-serving institutions (HSIs), emerging HSIs and non-HSIs. In A. Núñez, S. Hurtado, & E. C. Galdeano (Eds.), *Hispanic-serving institutions advancing research and transformative practice* (pp. 101–120). New York, NY: Routledge.

Dayton, B., Gonzalez-Vasquez, N., Martinez, C. R. & Plum, C. (2004). Hispanic-serving institutions through the eyes of students and administrators. In A. M. Ortiz (Ed.),. Addressing the unique needs of Latino American students (pp. 29–40). *New Directions for Student Services, No. 105*. San Francisco, CA: Jossey-Bass.

Delgado Bernal, D. (1997). *Chicana school resistance and grassroots leadership: Providing an alternative history of the 1968 East Los Angeles blowouts.* (PhD dissertation), University of California–Los Angeles.

de los Santos, A. G. & de los Santos, G. E. (2003). Hispanic-serving institutions in the 21st century: Overview, challenges, and opportunities. *Journal of Hispanic Higher Education, 2*(4) 377–387.

de Onís, C. M. (2017). What's in an "x"?: An exchange about the politics of "Latinx." *Chiricú Journal: Latina/o Literatures, Arts, and Cultures, 1*(2), 78-91.

Dill, B. T., & Zambrana, R. E. (2009). *Emerging intersections: Race, class, and gender in theory, policy, and practice*. New Brunswick, NJ: Rutgers University Press.

Dreid, N., & Najmabadi, S. (2016, December 13). Here's a rundown of the latest campus-climate incidents since Trump's election. *The Chronicle of Higher Education*. Retrieved from https://www.chronicle.com/blogs/ticker/heres-a-rundown-of-the-latest-campus-climate-incidents-since-trumps-election/115553

Duke, E. C. (2017). *Memorandum on rescission of Deferred Action for Childhood Arrivals (DACA)*. Retrieved from https://www.dhs.gov/news/2017/09/05/memorandum-rescission-daca

Erikson, E. H. (1959/1994). *Identity and the life cycle*. New York, NY: W.W. Norton & Company.

Félix-Ortiz de la Garza, M., Newcomb, M. D. & Myers, H. F. (1995). A multidimensional measure of cultural identity for Latino and Latina adolescents. In A.M. Padilla (Ed.), *Hispanic psychology critical issues in theory and research* (pp. 26–42). Thousand Oaks, CA: Sage.

Ferdman, B. M. & Gallegos, P. I. (2001). Racial identity development and Latinos in the United States. In C. L. Wijeyesinghe and B. W. Jackson III (Eds.), *New perspectives on racial identity development: A theoretical and practical anthology*, (pp. 32–66). New York, NY: New York University Press.

Fry, R. & Lopez, M. H. (2012). *Hispanic student enrollments reach new highs in 2011.* Washington DC: Pew Hispanic Center. Retrieved from http://www.pewhispanic.org/files/2012/08/Hispanic-Student-Enrollments-Reach-New-Highs-in-2011_FINAL.pdf

Garcia-Navarro, L. (2015, August 27). Hispanic or Latino? A guide for the U.S. presidential campaign. *NPR*. Retrieved from http://www.npr.org/sections/parallels/2015/08/27/434584260/hispanic-or-latino-a-guide-for-the-u-s-presidential-campaign

Garza, K. K., Bain, S. F., & Kupczynski, L. (2014). Resiliency, self-efficacy, and persistence of college seniors in higher education. *Research in Higher Education Journal, 26*, 1–19.

Gasman, M. (2008). Minority-serving institutions: A historical backdrop. In M. Gasman, B. Baez, & C. S. V. Turner (Eds.), *Understanding minority-serving institutions* (pp. 18–27). Albany, NY: State University of New York Press.

Gimenez, M. E. (1989). Latino/"Hispanic"—Who needs a name? The case against a standardized terminology. *International Journal of Health Services, 19*(3), 557–571.

Gloria, A. M. (1997). Chicana academic persistence creating a university-based community. *Education and Urban Society, 30*(1), 107–121.

Gloria, A. M. & Castellanos, J. (2003). Latina/o and African American students at predominantly white institutions: A psychosociocultural perspective of cultural congruity, campus climate, and academic persistence. In J. Castellanos & L. Jones (Eds.), *The majority in the minority: Expanding the representation of Latina/o faculty, administrators, and students in higher education* (pp. 71–94). Sterling, VA: Stylus.

Gloria, A.M. & Robinson Kurpius, S.E. (1996). The validation of the cultural congruity scale and the university environment scale with Chicano/a students. *Hispanic Journal of Behavioral Sciences, 18*(4) 533–549.

Golash-Boza, T., & William Darity, J. (2008). Latino racial choices: The effects of skin colour and discrimination on Latinos' and Latinas' self-identification. *Ethnic and Racial Studies, 31*(5), 899–934.

Gurin, P., Dey, E. L., Hurtado, S., & Gurin, G. (2002). Diversity and higher education: Theory and impact on educational outcomes. *Harvard Educational Review, 72*(3), 330–366.

Gutierrez, D. G. (1995). *Walls and mirrors: Mexican Americans, Mexican immigrants, and the politics of ethnicity*. Berkeley, CA: University of California Press.

Guzman, B. (2000). *The Hispanic population: Census 2000 brief*. Current Population Reports, C2KBR/01-3. Washington DC: U.S. Census Bureau.

Hamrick, F. A. & Stage, F. K. (2004). College predisposition at high-risk minority enrollment, low-income schools. *The Review of Higher Education, 27*(2), 151–168.

Harris, F. I. (2010). College men's meanings of masculinities and contextual influences: Toward a conceptual model. *Journal of College Student Development, 51*(3), 297–318.

Haywood, J. M. (2017). "Latino spaces have always been the most violent": Afro-Latino collegians perceptions of colorism and Latino intragroup marginalization. *International Journal of Qualitative Studies in Education, 30*(8), 759–782.

Hernández, E. (2012). The journey towards developing political consciousness through activism for Mexican American women. *Journal of College Student Development, 53*(5), 680–702.

Hernández, E. (2016). Utilizing critical race theory to examine race/ethnicity, racism, and power in student development theory and research. *Journal of College Student Development, 57*(2), 168–180.

Hernández, E. (2017). Critical theoretical perspectives. In J. Schuh, V. Torres, & S. R. Jones (Eds.), *Student services: A handbook for the profession,* (6th ed.), (pp. 205–219). San Francisco, CA: Jossey-Bass.

Hernández, T. K. (2003). "Too Black to be Latino/a:" Blackness and Blacks as foreigners in Latino Studies. *Latino Studies, 1*(1), 152–159.

Hoover, E. (2001, July 13). The first class of Gates scholars. *The Chronicle of Higher Education, 47*(44), pp. A34–36.

Hu, L. & Bentler, P. M. (1999). Cutoff criteria for fit indexes in covariance structure analysis: Convention criteria versus new alternatives. *Structural Equation Modeling: A Multidisciplinary Journal, 6*, 1–55.

Hurtado, S., Carter, D. F., & Spuler, A. (1996). Latino student transition to college. *Research in Higher Education, 37*(2), 135–157.

Hurtado, S., Milem, J., Clayton-Pedersen, A., & Allen, W. (1999). Enacting diverse learning environments. *ASHE-ERIC Higher Education Report, 26*(8). Washington DC: The George Washington University.

Immerwahr, J. (2003). *With diploma in hand: Hispanic high school seniors talk about their future.* San Jose, CA: National Center for Public Policy and Higher Education and Public Agenda.

Johnson-Bailey, J. (1999). The ties that bind and the shackles that separate: Race, gender, class, and color in a research process. *Qualitative Studies in Education, 12*(6), 659–670.

Johnston-Guerrero, M. P. (2016). Embracing the messiness: Critical and diverse perspectives on racial and ethnic identity development. *New Directions for Student Services, 154*, 43–55.

Jones, S. R. (2009). Constructing identities at the intersections: An autoethnographic exploration of multiple dimensions of identity. *Journal of College Student Development, 50*(3), 287–304.

Jones, S. R. (2010). Getting to the complexities of identity: The contributions of an autoethnographic and intersectional approach. In M. B. Baxter Magolda, E. G. Creamer, & P. S. Meszaros (Eds.), *Development and assessment of self-authorship: Exploring the concept across cultures* (pp. 223–243). Sterling, VA: Stylus.

Jones, S. R. & Abes, E. S. (2013). *Identity development of college students: Advancing frameworks for multiple dimensions of identity.* San Francisco, CA: Jossey Bass.

Jones, S. R., Kim, Y. C., & Skendall, K. C. (2012). (Re-)Framing authenticity: Considering multiple social identities using autoethnographic and intersectional approaches. *The Journal of Higher Education, 83*(5), 698–724.

Jones, S. R., & Stewart, D.-L. (2016). Evolution of student development theory. *New Directions for Student Services, 154*, 17–28.

Jöreskog, K. G. & Sörbom, D. (2001). *LISREL 8.50.* Lincolnwood, IL: Scientific Software International, Inc.

Keefe, S. E. & Padilla, A. M. (1987). *Chicano ethnicity.* Albuquerque, NM: University of Mexico Press.

Kegan, R. K. (1982). *The evolving self problem and process in human development.* Cambridge, MA: Harvard University Press.

Kewal Ramani, A., Gilbertson, L., Fox, M., & Provasnik, S. (2007). *Status and trends in the education of racial and ethnic minorities* (NCES 2007-039). National Center for Education Statistics, Institute of Education Sciences, U.S. Department of Education, Washington DC.

King, P. M. & Baxter Magolda, M. B. (2005). A developmental model of intercultural maturity. *Journal of College Student Development, 46*(6) 571–592.

Knight, G. P., Bernal, M. E., Garza, C. A. & Cota, M. K. (1993). A social cognitive model of the development of ethnic identity and ethnically-based behaviors. In M. E. Bernal & G. P. Knight (Eds.), *Ethnic identity formation and transmission among Hispanics and other minorities*, (pp. 213–234). Albany, NY: State University of New York Press.

Kroger, J. (2004). *Identity and adolescence: The balance between self and other* (3rd eds.). London, UK: Routledge.

Krogstad, J. M., & Lopez, M. H. (2014). *Hispanic nativity shift: U.S. births drive population growth as immigration stalls.* Available from http://www.pewhispanic.org/2014/04/29/hispanic-nativity-shift/

Kuh, G. D., Kinzie, J., Buckley, J. A., Bridges, B. K., & Hayek, J. C. (2007). Piecing together the student success puzzle: Research, propositions, and recommendations. *ASHE Higher Education Report, 32*(5). San Francisco, CA: Jossey-Bass.

Kuh, G. D., Kinzie, J., Schuh, J. H., & Whitt, E. J. (2011). *Student success in college: Creating conditions that matter.* San Francisco, CA: John Wiley & Sons.

Laden, B. V. (2001). Hispanic-serving institutions: Myths and realities. *Peabody Journal of Education, 76*(1), 73–92.

Leech, N. L., Barrett, K. C. & Morgan, G. A. (2005). *SPSS for intermediate statistics use and interpretation,* (2nd ed.) Mahwah, NJ: Erlbaum.

Levy, M. & Wright, M. (2016, June 9). Americans aren't biased against Latino immigration. Here's what they actually fear. *The Washington Post.* Retrieved from https://www.washingtonpost.com/news/monkey-cage/wp/2016/06/09/americans-arent-biased-against-latino-immigration-heres-what-they-actually-fear/?utm_term=.d9fa469abac0

Lincoln, Y. S. and Guba, E. G. (1985). *Naturalistic inquiry.* Thousand Oaks, CA: Sage.

Magee, J. C., & Smith, P. K. (2013). The social distance theory of power. *Personality and Social Psychology Review, 17*(2) 158–186.

Marcia, J. E. (2002). Identity and psychosocial development in adulthood. *Identity: An International Journal of Theory and Research, 2*(1), 7–28.

Marin, G. (1993). Influences of acculturation and familialism and self-identification among Hispanics. In M. E. Bernal & G. P. Knight (Eds). *Ethnic identity formation and transmission among Hispanics and other minorities* (pp. 181–196). Albany, NY: State University of New York Press.

Marin, G., Sabogal, F., Marin, B. V., Otero-Sabogal, R., & Perez-Stable, E. J. (1987). Development of a short acculturation scale for Hispanics. *Hispanic Journal of Behavioral Sciences, 9*(2), 183–205.

Martinez, G. F., & Deil-Amen, R. (2015). College for all Latinos? The role of high school messages in facing college challenges. *Teachers College Record, 117,* 1–50.

Martinez, S., Torres, V., Wallace White, L., Medrano, C. Robledo, A. and Hernandez, E. (2012). The influence of family dynamics on racial/ethnic identity among adult Latinas. *Journal of Adult Development, 19,* 190–200.

McMillan, J. H. & Schumacher, S. (2001). *Research in education,* (5th ed.). New York, NY: Addison Wesley Longman.

Mena, F. J., Padilla, A. M., & Maldonado, M. (1987). Acculturative stress and specific coping strategies among immigrant and later generation college students. *Hispanic Journal of Behavioral Sciences, 9*(2), 207–225.

Molina, A. (2016, August 31). *Latina, Latino, Latinx. What is the new term Latinx?* Available from https://www.naspa.org/constituent-groups/kcs/latinx-a-o/history

Murguia, E., Padilla, R. V., & Pavel, M. (1991). Ethnicity and the concept of social integration in Tinto's model of institutional departure. *Journal of College Student Development, 32,* 433–439.

National Center for Education Statistics. (2010). *Status and Trends in the Education of Racial and Ethnic Minorities, Table 23.2* (NCES 2010-015). Washington DC: U.S Department of Education, Institute of Education Sciences.

National Center for Education Statistics (2012). *Fast facts: Degrees conferred by sex and race, the condition of education 2012, Table A-47-2.* (NCES 2012-045). Washington DC: U.S. Department of Education, Institute of Education Sciences. Retrieved from https://nces.ed.gov/fastfacts/display.asp?id=72

National Student Survey of Student Engagement (NSSE). *Home page.* Retrieved from www.http://nsse.indiana.edu

Nelson, C., & Tienda, M. (1997). The structuring of Hispanic ethnicity: Historical and contemporary perspectives. In M. Romero, P. Hondagneu-Sotelo (Eds.), *Challenging fronteras: Structuring Latina and Latino lives in the U.S.* (pp. 7–29). New York, NY: Routledge.

Nelson Laird, T. F., Bridges, B. K., Morelon-Quainoo, C. L., Williams, J. M., & Salinas Holmes, M. (2007). African American and Hispanic student engagement at minority serving and predominantly White institutions. *Journal of College Student Development, 48*(1), 39–56.

Nora, A. (1987). Determinants of retention among Chicano college students: A structural model. *Research in Higher Education, 26*, 31–59.

Nora, A. & Cabrera, A. F. (1996). The role of perception of prejudice and discrimination on the adjustment of minority students to college. *The Journal of Higher Education, 67*(2), 119–148.

Nora, A., Kraemer, B. & Itzen, R. (1997). *Persistence among non-traditional Hispanic college students: A causal model.* Presented at the Association for the Study of Higher Education, Albuquerque, NM. ED 415 824.

Núñez, A., Crisp, G. & Elizondo, D. (2015). Hispanic-serving community colleges and their role in Hispanic transfer. In A. Núñez, S. Hurtado, & E. C. Galdeano (Eds.), *Hispanic-serving institutions advancing research and transformative practice* (pp. 47–81). New York, NY: Routledge.

Oboler, S. (1992). The politics of labeling: Latino/a cultural identities of self and others. *Latin American perspectives, 75*, 18–36.

Oboler, S. (1995). *Ethnic labels, Latino lives: Identity and the politics of (re)presentation in the United States.* Minneapolis, MN: University of Minnesota Press.

Ogunwole, S. U., Drewery, Jr., M. P., & Rios-Vargas, M. (2012). *The population with a bachelor's degree or higher by race and Hispanic origin: 2006-2010. American Community Survey.* Washington DC: U.S. Census Bureau.

Passel, J. S., & Cohn, D. (2008, February). *U.S. population projections: 2005-2050.* Washington DC: Pew Research Center. Available from http://www.pewhispanic.org/files/reports/85.pdf

Patton, L. D., Renn, K. A., Guido, F. M., & Quaye, S. J. (2016). *Student development in college: Theory, research, and practice* (3rd ed.). San Francisco, CA: Jossey-Bass.

Pérez Huber, L., Vélez, V.N., & Solórzano, D.G. (2014, October) The growing educational equity gap for California's Latina/o students. *Latino Policy & Issues Brief*, No. 29. Available from http://files.eric.ed.gov/fulltext/ED559368.pdf

Pew Research Center. (2013). *Hispanic or Latino? Many don't care, except in Texas.* Washington DC: Pew Research Center. Available from http://www.pewresearch.org/fact-tank/2013/10/28/in-texas-its-hispanic-por-favor/

Phinney, J. S. (1990). Ethnic identity in adolescents and adults: Review of research. *Psychological Bulletin, 108*(3), 499–514.

Phinney, J. S. (1992). The multigroup ethnic identity measure. *Journal of Adolescent Research, 7*(2), 156–176.

Phinney, J. S. (1993). A three-stage model of ethnic identity development in adolescence. In M. E. Bernal, & G. P. Knight (Eds.), *Ethnic identity formation and transmission among Hispanic and other minorities* (pp. 61–79). Albany, NY: State University of New York Press.

Quintana, S. M. (2007). Racial and ethnic identity: Developmental perspectives and research. *Journal of Counseling Psychology, 54*(3), 259.

Rendon, L. I., Jalomo, R. E., & Nora, A. (2000). Theoretical considerations in the study of minority student retention in higher education. In J. M. Braxton (Ed.), *Reworking the student departure puzzle* (pp. 127–156). Nashville, TN: Vanderbilt University Press.

Ruiz, A. S. (1990). Ethnic identity: Crisis and resolution. *Journal of Multicultural Counseling and Development, 18*, 29–40.

Salinas, C., & Lozano, A. (2017, November 16). Mapping and recontextualizing the evolution of the term Latinx: An environmental scanning in higher education. *Journal of Latinos and Education*, 1–17. Retrieved from http://www.tandfonline.com/doi/full/10.1080/15348431.2017.1390464?src=recsys

Santiago, D. A., Taylor, M., & Calderón Galdeano, E. (2016). *From capacity to success: HSI's, Title V, and Latino students.* Washington DC: *Excelencia* in Education. Retrieved from http://www.edexcelencia.org/research/capacity

Schmidt, P. (2003, November 28). Academe's Hispanic future. *The Chronicle of Higher Education, 50*(14), A8–12.

Selingo, J. (2004, September 10). Two weeks at 'Philadelphia public.' *The Chronicle of Higher Education, 51*(3), A56.

Smedley, A., & Smedley, B. (2005). Race as biology is fiction, race as a social problem is real: Anthropological and historical perspectives on the social construction of race. *American Psychologist 60*(1), 16–26.

Solórzano, D. G. (1998). Critical race theory, race and gender microagressions, and the experience of Chicana and Chicano scholars. *Qualitative Studies in Education, 11*(1), 121–136.

Steele, C. M., & Aronson, J. (1995). Stereotype threat and the intellectual test performance of African Americans. *Journal of Personality and Social Psychology, 69*(5), 797–811.

Stepler, R., & Brown, A. (2016). *Statistical portrait of Hispanics in the United States.* Washington DC: Pew Research Center. Retrieved from http://www.pewhispanic.org/2016/04/19/statistical-portrait-of-hispanics-in-the-united-states-key-charts/

Strauss, A. and Corbin, J. (1998). *Basics of qualitative research techniques and procedures for developing grounded theory.* (2nd ed.). Thousand Oaks, CA: Sage.

Strauss, L. C., & Volkwein, J. F. (2004). Predictors of student commitment at two-year and four-year institutions. *The Journal of Higher Education, 75*(2), 203–227.

Strmic-Pawl, H. V., Jackson, B. A., & Garner, S. (2017). Race counts: Racial and ethnic data on U.S. Census and the implications for tracking inequality. *Sociology of Race and Ethnicty*, 1–13. Retrieved from https://doi.org/10.1177/2332649217742869

Suarez-Balcazar, Y., Orellana-Damacela, L., Portillo, N., Rowan, J. M., & Andrews-Guillen, C. (2003). Experiences of differential treatment among college students of color. *Journal of Higher Education, 74*(4), 428–444.

Tanaka, G. (2002). Higher education's self-reflexive turn toward an intercultural theory of student development. *The Journal of Higher Education, 73*, 263–296.

Tatum, B. D. (1997). *Why are all the Black kids sitting together in the cafeteria?* New York, NY: Basic Books.

Taylor, P., Kochhar, R., Morin, R., Wang, W., Dockterman, D., & Medina, J. (2009). *America's changing workforce: Recession turns a graying office grayer.* A Social & Demographic Trends Report. Washington DC: Pew Research Center. Retrieved from http://www.pewsocialtrends.org/files/2010/10/americas-changing-workforce.pdf

Therrien, M. & Ramirez, R. R. (2000). *The Hispanic population in the United States: March 2000*. Current Population Reports, P20-535. Washington DC: U.S. Census Bureau.

Tierney, W. G. (1992). An anthropological analysis of student participation in college. *The Journal of Higher Education, 63*, 603–618.

Tierney, W. G. (2000). Power, identity, and the dilemma of college student departure. In J. M. Braxton (Ed.), *Reworking the student departure puzzle* (pp. 213–234). Nashville, TN: Vanderbilt University Press.

Tinto, V. (1993). *Leaving college: Rethinking the causes and cures of student attrition.* Chicago, IL: University of Chicago Press.

Torres, V. (1999). Validation of a bicultural orientation model for Hispanic college students. *Journal of College Student Development, 40*(3), 285–299.

Torres, V. (2003a) Influences on ethnic identity development of Latino college students in the first two years of college. *Journal of College Student Development, 44*, 532–547.

Torres, V. (2003b). Student diversity and academic services: Balancing the needs of all students. In G. L. Kramer (Ed.), *Student academic services an integrated approach* (pp. 333–351). San Francisco, CA: Jossey-Bass.

Torres, V. (2004a) Familial influences on the identity development of Latino first year students. *Journal of College Student Development, 45*, 457–469.

Torres, V (2004b). The diversity among U.S.: Puerto Ricans, Cubans, Caribbean, Central and South Americans. In A.M. Ortiz, (Ed.), Addressing the unique needs of Latino/a American students. *New Directions for Student Services,* (Vol. 105, pp. 516). San Francisco, CA: Jossey-Bass.

Torres, V. (2006). A mixed method study testing data-model fit of a retention model for Latino/a students at urban universities. *Journal of College Student Development, 47*(3), 299–318.

Torres, V. (2009). The developmental dimensions of recognizing racism. *Journal of College Student Development, 50*(5), 504–520.

Torres, V. (2011). Perspectives on identity development. In J. H. Schuh, S. R. Jones and S. R. Harper (Eds.), *Student services: A handbook for the profession*, (5th ed.). (pp. 187–206). San Francisco, CA: Jossey Bass.

Torres, V., & Baxter Magolda, M. B. (2004). Reconstructing Latino identity: The influence of cognitive development on the ethnic identity process of Latino students. *Journal of College Student Development, 45*(3), 333–347.

Torres, V., & Delgado-Romero, E. (2008). Defining Latino/a identity through late adolescent development. In K. L. Kraus (Ed.), *Lifespan development theories in action: A case study approach for counseling professionals* (pp. 363–388). Boston, MA: Lahaska Press.

Torres, V., & De Sawal, D. (2004). *The role environment plays in retaining Latino students at urban universities*. NASPA Convention, 2004, Denver: CO.

Torres, V., & Hernandez, E. (2007). The influence of ethnic identity on self-authorship: A longitudinal study of Latino/a college students. *Journal of College Student Development, 48*, 558–573.

Torres, V., & Hernandez, E. (2009). Influence of an identified advisor/mentor on urban Latino students' college experience. *Journal of College Student Retention, 11*(1), 141–160.

Torres, V., Howard-Hamilton, M., & Cooper, D. L. (2003) Identity development of diverse populations: Implications for teaching and practice. *ASHE/ERIC Higher Education Report, 29*. San Francisco, CA: Jossey Bass.

Torres, V., Jones, S. R., & Renn, K. A. (2009). Identity development among theories in student affairs: Origins, current status, and new approaches. *Journal of College Student Development, 50*(6) 577–596.

Torres, V., Martinez, S., Wallace, L., Medrano, C., Robledo, A., & Hernandez, E. (2012). The connections between Latino ethnic identity and adult experiences. *Adult Education Quarterly*, 62(1) 3–18.

Torres, V., Reiser, A., LePeau, L., Davis, L., & Ruder, J. (2006). A model of first-generation Latino/a college students' approach to seeking academic information. *NACADA Journal 26*(2) 65–70.

Torres, V., Winston, R. B. Jr., & Cooper, D. L. (2003). The effect of geographic location, institutional type, and stress on Hispanic students' cultural orientation. *NASPA Journal, 40*(2), 153–172. Retrieved from http://publications.naspa.org/naspajournal/vol40/iss2/art10

U.S. Census Bureau. (2001). The Hispanic Population: 2000. Washington DC: US Department of Commerce. Retrieved from https://www.census.gov/prod/2001pubs/c2kbr01-3.pdf

U.S. Census Bureau. (2011a). *Statistical Abstract of the United States: 2012*. Washington DC: U.S Department of Commerce. Retrieved from http://www2.census.gov/library/publications/2011/compendia/statab/131ed/2012-statab.pdf

U.S. Census Bureau. (2011b). *The Hispanic population: 2010.* Washington DC: U.S. Department of Commerce. Retrieved from https://www.census.gov/prod/cen2010/briefs/c2010br-04.pdf

U.S. Census Bureau. (2015). *Projections of the size and composition of the U.S. population: 2014 to 2060.* Washington DC: U.S. Department of Commerce. Retrieved from http://census.gov/content/dam/Census/library/publications/2015/demo/p25-1143.pdf

Villalpando, O. (2002). The impact of diversity and multiculturalism on all students: Findings from a national study. *NASPA Journal, 40*(1), 124–144.

Whitt, E. J. (2005). *Promoting student success: What student affairs can do* (Occasional Paper No. 5). Bloomington, IN: Indiana University Center for Postsecondary Research.

Zalaquett, C. P. & Lopez, A. D. (2006). Learning from the stories of successful undergraduate Latina/Latino students: The importance of mentoring. *Mentoring & Tutoring, 14*(3), 337–353.

Zavella, P. (1991). Reflections on diversity among Chicanas. *Frontiers: A Journal of Women Studies, 12*(2), 73–85.

ABOUT THE AUTHORS

Vasti Torres is a professor in the Center for the Study of Higher and Postsecondary Education (CSHPE) at the University of Michigan. Previously she was the dean of the College of Education at the University of South Florida and professor and director of the Center for Postsecondary Research (CPR) in the School of Education at Indiana University. Before becoming a faculty member, she had 15 years of experience in administrative positions, most recently serving as associate vice provost and dean for enrollment and student services at Portland State University. She has been the principal investigator for several grants including a multi-year grant investigating the choice to stay in college for Latinx students, as well as a multi-year grant looking at the experiences of working college students. She has worked on several community college initiatives including Achieving the Dream and Rural Community College Initiative. She was the associate editor of the *Journal of College Student Development* from 2008 to 2015. In 2007–2008 she became the first Latina president of a national student services association, the American College Personnel Association (ACPA). In 2019 she began her term as vice president for Division J: Postsecondary Education for the American Educational Research Association (AERA). She received the Contribution to Knowledge Award from both ACPA and NASPA. She was also honored as a Diamond Honoree, Senior Scholar, Wise Woman, and received the Latino Network John Hernandez Leadership Award by ACPA. Other honors include the Professional Achievement Alumni Award from the University of Georgia, and Program Associate for the National Center for Policy in Higher Education. In 2008 she received the Indiana University Trustees Teaching Award. In 2011–2012 she served as a Fulbright Specialist in South Africa. Torres is a graduate of Stetson University and holds a PhD from the University of Georgia.

Ebelia Hernández is an associate professor in the School of Education at Rutgers University. Her areas of research focus on Latina/o/x student engagement and student development theory, specifically the interconnections between student activism and identity development. She was selected as a

Rutgers University Chancellor's Scholar for 2016–2021. Additional honors and awards include the ACPA Annuit Coeptis–Emerging Professional, ACPA Emerging Scholar, and American Association of Hispanics in Higher Education faculty fellow. She was also a finalist for NASPA's Melvene D. Hardee Dissertation of the Year. She served on the editorial board for the *Journal of College Student Development* from 2010 to 2016. Hernández earned her PhD in higher education from Indiana University; MS in Counseling from California State University, Northridge; and BA in English from California State University, Chico.

Sylvia Martinez is an associate professor in educational leadership and policy studies and the Latino Studies program at Indiana University-Bloomington. Her research examines two lines of inquiry. First, she focuses on the high school to college transition among Latinx youth, particularly where and how Latinx students access information about college and universities. Second, her work explores how Latinx ethnic identity among undergraduates impacts participation at campus cultural centers. Martinez earned her undergraduate degree from Pomona College and her PhD in sociology from the University of Chicago.

INDEX

Index legend: all single names are pseudonyms.

(*Continued from preceding page*)

Sentipensante (Sensing/Thinking) Pedagogy

Educating for Wholeness, Social Justice and Liberation

Laura I. Rendón

Foreword by Mark Nepo

"In this visionary study, Rendón lays the groundwork for a pedagogy that bridges the gap between mind and heart to lead students and educators toward a new conception of teaching and learning. Grounding her work in interviews of scholars who are already transforming the educational landscape, Rendón invites the reader to join a burgeoning movement toward more inclusive classrooms that honor each learner's identity and support education for social justice. Her book is vital reading for anyone seeking to create more inclusive institutions for students and teachers alike." ***—Diversity & Democracy (AAC&U)***

"This masterpiece . . . is about inclusion, one in which faculty and students become one in recognizing and accepting their responsibility [for] social justice and liberation. All who [teach] must read this book. It should be considered required material in diversity, social sciences, and education courses. If I must select a word to describe this book, it would be ¡ *Magnífico!*" ***—Hispanic Outlook in Higher Education***

Stylus

22883 Quicksilver Drive
Sterling, VA 20166-2019

Subscribe to our e-mail alerts: www.Styluspub.com

(Continued from preceding page)

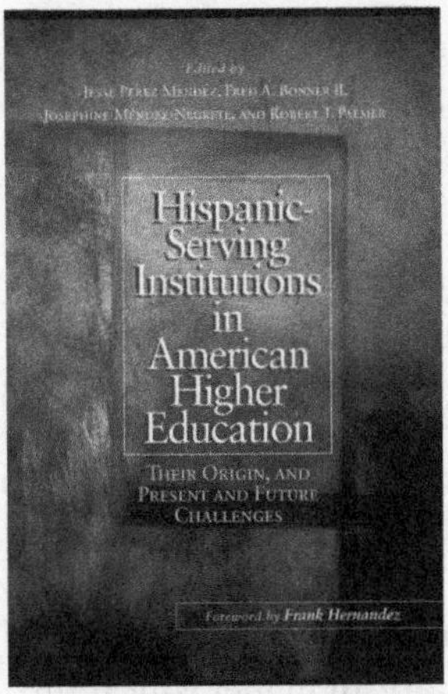

Hispanic-Serving Institutions in American Higher Education

Their Origin, and Present and Future Challenges

Edited by Jesse Perez Mendez, Fred A. Bonner II, Josephine Méndez-Negrete, and Robert T. Palmer

Foreword by Frank Hernandez

This is the first book to exclusively address Hispanic-serving institutions (HSIs), filling a major gap in both the research on these institutions and in our understanding of their approaches to learning and their role in supporting all students while focusing on Hispanic students.

Written by leading and rising scholars on HSIs, this book offers insight into the complexity of these institutions. It not only addresses historic policy origins but also describes the experiences of various student populations served, faculty issues (e.g., governance, diversity, work/life experience, etc.), and the impact of student affairs in advancing student development, as well as considers funding and philanthropy efforts. The book also critically examines challenges that many of these institutions face—disjointed mission statements regarding support of their Latino/a student populations, governance structures that support the status quo, and the financial incentive to achieve HSI designation that may not correlate with enhancing the climate for Latinos. This book touches on the many facets of HSIs, painting an organic mosaic of institutions in a position to advance Latino postsecondary progress, chronicling the contemporary challenges that these institutions face while also looking to their future.

(Continues on preceding page)

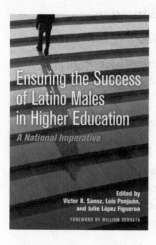

(Continues on preceding page)